Sarah and Donald Sykes

18. xii. 2007

Know Your New Zealand ...

Trees

Lawrie Metcalf

NEW
HOLLAND

First published in 2006 by New Holland Publishers (NZ) Ltd
Auckland • Sydney • London • Cape Town

www.newhollandpublishers.co.nz

218 Lake Road, Northcote, Auckland, New Zealand
Unit 1, 66 Gibbes Street, Chatswood, NSW 2067, Australia
86–88 Edgware Road, London W2 2EA, United Kingdom
80 McKenzie Street, Cape Town 8001, South Africa

Managing editor: Matt Turner
Editor: Brian O'Flaherty/Punaromia
Design and layout: Julie McDermid/Punaromia
Cover design: Nick Turzynski, redinc

National Library of New Zealand Cataloguing-in-Publication Data

Metcalf, L. J. (Lawrence James), 1928-
Know your New Zealand trees / Lawrie Metcalf.
ISBN: 978 1 86966 098 7
1. Trees—New Zealand. 2. Trees—New Zealand—
Identification. I. Title.
582.160993—dc 22

10 9 8 7 6 5 4 3 2

Front cover photographs: clockwise from left: pohutukawa (Bob McCree), rimu, kauri,
kahikatea. Back cover photographs, from top: kahikatea, manuka, rimu, cabbage tree.

Colour reproduction by Pica Digital Pte Ltd, Singapore
Printed by Tien Wah Press (Pte) Ltd

Contents

Introduction

For anyone with an interest in our native trees, this book serves as an introduction to a richly satisfying subject and as a handbook for further study. There are some 260 species of trees native to New Zealand (compare this with fewer than 30 species native to the British Isles). This book does not cover all of them, nor the various exotic species that have been introduced since the early days of settlement, but it illustrates and describes the more common natives.

Eighty-one of our trees have been selected for inclusion here. In many instances they have been chosen because they are the most interesting. Some are included because they are the species more likely to be encountered in various parts of the country. Others are much more restricted in their distribution and are unlikely to be noticed when travelling around New Zealand. Some species are naturally distributed only in certain latitudes. The kauri, for instance, occurs only north of latitude 38 degrees. The nikau palm is another example of a tree with a restricted distribution, albeit a wider one: it is found in coastal, lowland and hilly forests throughout the North Island, but it reaches its southern limit in the South Island at Banks Peninsula on the east coast and Wanganui Bluff on the west. It is also found on the Chatham Islands.

Practically all of New Zealand's trees are evergreen (which is in marked contrast to many of the more temperate forests of the northern hemisphere, except for the tropics); fewer than about 12 native species are deciduous or partially deciduous. Some, such as the kowhai (the various species of *Sophora*), are mainly deciduous at flowering time while others are only deciduous in colder parts of the country or at higher altitudes.

To the untrained eye New Zealand's native trees can be unfamiliar and difficult to identify or classify. Not only is there a great number of species representing a diverse range of plant families, but they also occur in a wide variety of forms. One distinct feature of our native trees is that quite a number of species undergo a marked juvenile stage, which may be so distinct from that of the adult tree that it is easy to believe them to be completely different species. The two species of lancewood are a case in point. Early 19th-century botanists did, in fact, believe the juveniles of these two species to be different species to those of the adult trees. As well as the variation caused by juvenility, many trees also show a great deal of regional variation in their general appearance.

New Zealand's geographic isolation and the particular composition of its native animal life have meant that, unlike those of most other forested regions in the world, its forests have evolved over thousands of years in the complete absence of browsing mammals. Among New Zealand's native animals only some of the smaller species of now extinct large, flightless birds (the moa) browsed in the forests, and, contrary to one popular theory, they appear not to have had any evolutionary effect on the forest vegetation. In fact, the absence of native browsers has greatly influenced the evolution of many native plants. In more recent times, the deliberate introduction of browsing mammals – deer, sheep, cattle, goats, wallabies and the brush-tailed possum – has in a comparatively brief time span dramatically altered the composition and nature of many of our indigenous forests.

Over 80 per cent of New Zealand's native plants are endemic (found nowhere else), which is regarded as a high degree (although some other southern hemisphere countries can also claim similar percentages of endemism).

Originally, some 80 per cent of New Zealand was covered with forest but the advent of human settlement, 800 or 900 years ago, began a slow but steady change to the amount of forest cover. For cultivating crops, the early Polynesian settlers originally attempted to use the traditional slash-and-burn techniques that are commonly used in tropical countries. Because of New Zealand's more temperate and seasonal climate, the cleared vegetation failed to regrow quickly enough so that such techniques did not work. This resulted in the deforestation of a large part of the south-eastern area of the North Island. For unknown reasons, large areas of the eastern South Island were also subject to burning by the early Polynesian inhabitants and that, along with climatic changes that occurred around that time, resulted in the forest cover never returning to those areas. By the beginning of the 19th century the remaining forest cover had been reduced to about 64 per cent. In the 19th and early 20th centuries the forest clearance was greatly accelerated following the arrival of the first European settlers, who required land for farming, timber production and settlement. Today, the amount of forest cover of the whole of New Zealand is probably no more than about 23 per cent.

When one considers the history of the last 200 years it is amazing, not that so little forest has survived, but that that so much still remains. Nowadays, the majority of our native forest areas are protected in national parks, scenic reserves, forest parks and other conservation land as well as those areas that may be under the control of local authorities or covenanted by the Queen Elizabeth the Second Trust. Numerous management and forest-restoration programmes are being undertaken, largely with the involvement of local people, voluntary groups and some businesses.

The question often arises as to how a tree is defined. The usual definition is 'any large, woody, perennial plant, with a distinct trunk, giving rise to branches or leaves at some distance from the ground'. This definition may be quite adequate for trees as they grow in forests, but it must also be borne in mind that trees can grow in many different habitats, often considerably removed from their usual forest habitat. The influence of habitat situations can make quite a difference to the ultimate size of many trees. For example, a tree that may grow to 12 m tall in the forest can be much smaller when in an exposed situation outside of the forest. Similarly, the broadleaf (*Griselinia littoralis*) may attain heights of 15 m or more in the forest, but it may often be seen growing on exposed rocky sites reaching a height of no more than a metre or so, and yet it is still regarded as a tree, even though it behaves as a shrub.

Forest types

Our native forests are broadly classified as rainforests and are divided into two main types: subtropical rainforest (known as rainforest proper) and subantarctic rainforest. Whether rainforest exists or not depends upon the number of rainy days per annum, and the total annual rainfall and not necessarily on the moisture content of the soil. Obviously, if the annual total of rainy days is too limited and the annual rainfall inadequate then rainforest cannot exist; consequently, there must be a great abundance of rainy days for rainforest to prevail.

Because the climate of present-day New Zealand is generally warm-temperate some authors refer to our subtropical rainforests as temperate rainforest. This does not take into account the fundamental tropical origins of these forests and their whole present aspect being that of a moist mountain forest in a tropical country such as in Indonesia, the Philippines or New Caledonia rather than the typical forests of the temperate zones.

Subtropical rainforest

New Zealand rainforest comprises a mixture of coniferous trees and broad-leaved evergreens. The coniferous trees have very ancient origins, over several millions of years, which go back to the former supercontinent of Gondwanaland. They belong to the Podocarpaceae and are commonly referred to as podocarps. Generally, they are tall trees that are either closely placed to form a close upper canopy or they may be more scattered, more or less as individual trees whose crowns rise clear of the surrounding canopy and which are then referred to as emergent trees. Our principal timber trees, rimu, miro, matai, kahikatea, totara and kauri, are all podocarps. Their presence gives the forest a very ancient and primeval aspect.

Another character that indicates the tropical origins of our forests is the fact that a number of species of the taller trees often develop buttresses at the bases of their trunks. The uppermost roots then extend, half buried or even raised above the ground, for quite some distance. Usually the larger trees support a variety of epiphytes (perching plants), often thick-stemmed lianes (climbing plants), orchids, mosses, liverworts and ferns. Another factor that provides a tropical or subtropical aspect is the abundance of tree ferns.

Subtropical rainforest was formerly found across most of the North Island and throughout much of the South Island, with the exception of parts of the drier eastern regions from Marlborough south to Central Otago. Stewart Island retains much of its original forest cover.

The composition of New Zealand's subtropical forest is naturally graded according to latitude, with some of the less hardy species progressively dropping out towards the higher latitudes farther south. The upshot of this is that some trees are predominantly North Island species and others typically South; there is, however, an interesting area of overlap in north-western Nelson and the Marlborough Sounds, where a number of the more typically North Island species reach the southern limit of their distribution.

Contained within New Zealand's subtropical rainforest there are several different forest types. The following are some of the main ones.

- **Kauri forest** once covered much of the northern part of the North Island northwards from Kawhia and the Coromandel Peninsula. Although kauri was the dominant tree, taraire also formed a large part of this forest. There was also a variety of other mixed trees and shrubs. Sadly, overzealous harvesting in the 19th and early 20th centuries decimated the formerly magnificent kauri forests.

- **Tawa forest** is dominated by the fast-growing tawa. It grows in localised pockets in various parts of the North Island, and is also present in the Marlborough Sounds and the north-western Nelson region.

- **Kahikatea forest** is unlike other types in that it grows in wet ground near rivers or in shallow swamps. It is dominated to a greater or lesser degree by the kahikatea, our tallest forest tree, which may appear in dense stands or in a more scattered manner, depending on the location. It was once one of the most common native trees, widespread in areas such as the Waikato, the King Country and Westland, but timber milling and land clearance have severely reduced its habitats.

- **(Northern) rata forest** is dominated by rata, also known as northern rata, which forms large trees up to 24 m tall that often contain epiphytic and climbing forest species. As well as being common in the North Island, it also occurs in parts of north-western Nelson and northern Westland.

- **Kamahi forest** is quite widespread, with kamahi being a common tree in lowland and montane forests, in the North Island, from the mid-Waikato and lower Coromandel southwards and throughout the South and Stewart Islands. Kamahi forest is especially common in parts of Westland and Stewart Island. Kamahi is one of the most common species to regenerate after forest has been cleared, with seedlings quickly invading any open spaces in the forest.

Subantarctic rainforest

The subantarctic rainforest is essentially temperate and is characterised by the presence of the various native species of southern beech or *Nothofagus*. Pure beech forests are more open than the subtropical forests, with fewer understorey species present, and they generally lack the diversity of species that occurs in the subtropical rainforest. Beech forests are characteristic of montane regions, above 300 m altitude, in the central and southern North and South Islands. Southern beech species can be found from the southern part of the Coromandel Peninsula to Southland. (The exception is N. *truncata*, the hard beech, which extends as far north as Mangonui.) Beeches are absent from Stewart Island. Although the beeches generally occur on the mountain ranges, one or two species may be common in lowland areas. Especially in the southern part of their range, as well as in the Marlborough Sounds, they also occur down to sea level. For some unknown reason, there are no beech species on Mt Taranaki in the North Island.

How to use this book

For convenience, the trees described in this book are listed according to the families to which they belong and are in currently accepted botanical order. The members of each family are also grouped together. Their scientific names include the genus (the first name) and species (the second name). Readers can see the relationships between the various species and genera and also those of closely related families. Where there is more than one genus in a plant family, the genera and species of each family are arranged in alphabetical order.

In the side panel are listed a couple of key features, the scientific name, alternative names in current use (former names are given in the main text), key Maori names, and the approximate average height of a mature tree in metres. The distribution maps indicate the parts of the country where each species may occur. They are a general guide only and not definitive; a species may not occur in all parts of the area indicated.

The main entry for each species includes a description of its general appearance, habit, foliage, flowers and fruit, as well as cultural or other uses.

Botanical terminology has been kept to a minimum, and to assist with understanding the meanings of those terms that are used, a glossary and some diagrams follow.

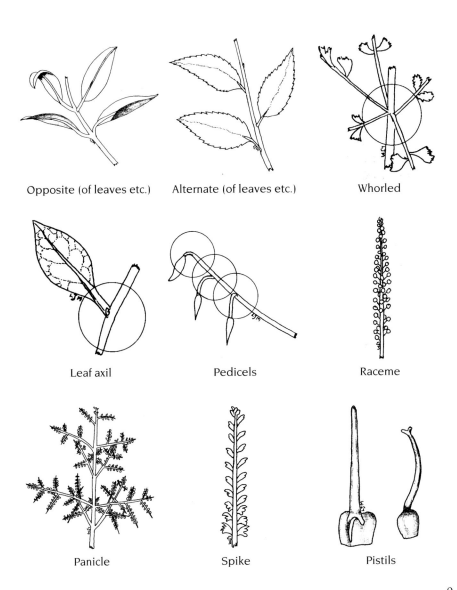

Opposite (of leaves etc.)   Alternate (of leaves etc.)   Whorled

Leaf axil   Pedicels   Raceme

Panicle   Spike   Pistils

Glossary

Alternate: (leaves) placed singly along a stem or axis, not in opposite pairs.

Appressed: (leaves) closely and flatly pressed against the surface of a stem.

Aril: an appendage to a seed, usually an outgrowth of the stalk of the ovule, and often pulpy or succulent.

Axil: (adjective: axillary) the upper angle, usually between leaf and stem.

Canopy: the layer of branches or upper storey in a community of forest trees.

Compound: particularly of leaves; composed of several, more or less similar, parts (leaflets) as opposed to simple.

Cone: the hardened, woody fruit of coniferous trees such as kauri.

Corolla: the inner whorl of floral parts, consisting of free or united petals.

Corymb: (adjective: corymbose) a more or less flat-topped raceme with its long-stalked outer flowers opening first.

Cupule: a cup-like structure at the bases of some fruits, especially of *Nothofagus* or southern beeches.

Deciduous: (trees) shedding all leaves in autumn, or (e.g. kowhai) shedding all or most of its leaves in the late spring before new growth begins.

Deflexed: bent sharply downwards.

Divaricate: (adjective: divaricated) trees or shrubs with their stiff stems and branchlets spreading at wide angles to become very tangled.

Drupe: a succulent fruit with the seed enclosed in a stony or bony covering.

Emergent: trees that tower above the general canopy of a forest and are usually scattered as individuals or groups of individuals.

Entire: mainly of leaves; refers to a continuous margin completely lacking in teeth, although hairs may be present.

Epiphyte: (adjective: epiphytic) a plant that grows or perches upon another but is not organically connected to it.

Flexuous: having a wavy or zigzag form.

Fluted: (bark) having rounded, shallow grooves or furrows running vertically up the trunk.

Glaucous: having a whitish or greyish appearance, but not necessarily due to a waxy or powdery bloom.

Incised: deeply and sharply, sometimes irregularly, cut.

Inflorescence: a general term for a collection of the flowering parts of a plant, or of the arrangement of the flowers.

Kernel: the edible seed of a nut or fruit within the shell or stone.

Lenticel: a corky spot on bark, which functions as a pore or breathing orifice.

Midrib: the main central vein of a leaf or organ.

Montane: those areas below the subalpine and alpine regions.

Panicle: a loose, irregularly branched inflorescence, often with many flowers.

Pellucid: transparent or translucent.

Perfect: a flower having both male and female elements present.

Petiole: (adjective: petiolate) the main stalk of a leaf.

Pinnate: (a compound leaf) with the parts or segments arranged either side of an axis, or midrib, as in a feather.

Pistil: the female reproductive part of a flower.

Pneumatophore: a specialised breathing root of the mangrove (*Avicennia*).

Pungent: (leaf) having a sharp point.

Raceme: (adjective: racemose) an inflorescence having several to many stalked flowers arranged along a single stem.

Ray floret: in Asteraceae or Compositae (the daisy family), one of the outer florets of the flower head which have strap-like corollas.

Receptacle: the enlarged uppermost part of the flower stalk on which the floral parts are borne.

Rhizome: an underground stem, usually spreading more or less horizontally.

Serrate: (leaves) with a saw-like margin.

Simple: (leaves) in one piece and not being divided into leaflets.

Sorus: (plural: sori) a cluster of sporangia (spore-containing structures) prominent on the fronds of most ferns.

Spike: an unbranched inflorescence on which the flowers do not have stalks but sit directly on the stem.

Sporangium: of ferns, a sac or other structure containing spores.

Strobilus: (plural: strobili) a cone-like structure containing the reproductive organs, especially the male or pollen-producing ones.

Style: the long, slender extension of the ovary bearing the stigma.

Subalpine: the lower areas of the alpine zone, above the tree line but below the true alpine zone, containing herbfields, fellfields etc.

Terminal: borne at the end of a stem and thus limiting its growth.

Terrestrial: plants that grow rooted into the ground.

Tomentum: a dense, matted covering of soft, appressed hairs.

Umbel: a cluster of individual flowers where several flower stalks arise from the same point.

Unisexual: of or relating to one sex.

Valve: any of the several parts that make up a dry, woody capsule and which generally splits open to release mature seeds.

Whorled: (an arrangement) having three or more parts or organs, at the same level, around an axis or stem.

Kahikatea

Although the kauri might be the mightiest of our forest trees, kahikatea is by far the tallest, and specimens over 60 m high have been measured. It normally has a very straight trunk and when growing as more scattered trees may tower over the surrounding forest. It may also form a complete canopy if growing in dense, pure stands as it does in some lowland areas. Kahikatea occurs in lowland forests throughout New Zealand, especially in swampy areas or on moist alluvial flats.

Generally, kahikatea has rather slender trunks that are topped with relatively small crowns so that it is usually a distinct and easily recognised tree. The trunk has a medium- to dark-grey bark which is smooth but scales off in largish flakes. Particularly when growing in wet or swampy areas, the base of the trunk is often fluted or buttressed, and sometimes it may also have exposed, long, thick roots.

On adult trees the small, scale-like leaves are sharply pointed and less appressed (flattened) to the branchlets than those of rimu, and are softer to touch. Its small, orange fruits comprise a swollen and fleshy footstalk or receptacle, on top of which is a black seed covered with a whitish, waxy bloom (see inset photo). Kahikatea trees do not necessarily fruit well every year but, when they do, the fruits will colour the trees so that they are quite reddish. New Zealand pigeons, tui and kaka feed on the fruits, and fallen fruits may often be seen on bush tracks.

Young and semi-adult trees are quite different from the adult but generally are easily recognised. Young trees have a very open habit of growth, while the semi-adults have a conical shape. In some areas, groups of semi-adult trees may often be seen on farmlands.

Kahikatea was formerly one of the most abundant trees, but milling for timber and land clearance greatly reduced the areas of kahikatea forest. Before the advent of cardboard cartons, its odourless timber was used for making butter boxes. It was also favoured for boat building but was seldom used for building construction because it was so readily attacked by the larvae of borer beetles. The sweet fruits of kahikatea were a favourite food of early Maori who would climb these lofty trees – often a dangerous task – to gather the fruits, which were put into baskets before being lowered to the ground on long ropes.

■ Pyramidal shape when young; pendulous branchlets.

■ Dark, brownish-grey, flaking bark.

Height: 18–30 m

Scientific Name: *Dacrydium cupressinum*

The one universal native timber tree that could be obtained from almost throughout the whole country and which provided timber that could be used for a wealth of purposes was rimu or, as it used to be called in earlier times, red pine. In addition, it is one of the most beautiful and graceful of our native forest trees. It is a true rainforest tree and sometimes forms complete canopies while in other situations it is an emergent tree towering above the rest of the forest.

One of the distinctive features of an adult rimu that enables it to be easily identified is the bark of mature trees. It is a dark, brownish-grey and scales off or peels off in quite long flakes. Apart from their bark, mature trees may be recognised by their rather spreading crowns of pendulous branchlets. Rimu attain heights of 18–30 m.

Young rimu trees form elegant, pyramidal trees with long, pendulous branchlets and they are often easily recognised in patches of young, regenerating forest. On these young trees the sharply pointed leaves are about 4–7 mm long by about 1 mm wide and they overlap all around the branchlet. That stage will persist for many years. Once the tree begins to assume adulthood, the leaves become smaller, more closely set and more appressed (flattened) to the branchlet (see inset photo). Unlike kahikatea, the leaves are prickly to touch.

The pollen cones or strobili usually are produced in ones and twos at the branchlet tips while only single female flowers are produced. The female flowers are followed by orange-scarlet fruits from which protrude the black seeds. Rimu trees do not necessarily flower every year but rather they may have a sporadic flowering followed, every few years (usually five to six years), by a really abundant flowering and fruiting.

Some standing rimu trees are estimated to be from 800 to 1000 years old. The cutting of trees on Crown land is now restricted so that only rimu on private land can be harvested for their timber. Maori used to harvest the fruits. The timber of rimu has been used for all kinds of building construction, furniture, joinery and general purposes. Rimu was formerly abundant in lowland and hilly forests throughout the North, South and Stewart Islands from sea level to about 600 m.

Hall's totara

New Zealand has two species of forest trees that are commonly referred to as totara. Hall's totara is also known as thin-bark totara because of its thin and papery, flaky, brown bark, as opposed to the thick and fibrous bark of the common totara. The trunks of Hall's totara are always quite smooth and that is one of the main distinguishing characters of the species.

While Hall's totara will attain quite large dimensions it does not reach the massive size of the common totara. It will grow to about 20 m or so in height and its trunk may be up to about 1.25 m in diameter. Its leaves are generally somewhat larger than those of the common totara, although that is not always such an obvious character. Especially on juvenile plants, they are even larger, often being up to 5 cm long, and they are often brownish-green (lower photo). The leaves of adult trees are sharply pointed, prickly to touch, and are generally 2–3 cm long by 3–4 mm wide.

The male and female flowers are produced separately in early summer. The male strobili (pollen cones) are about 2.5 cm long and they normally fall from the tree soon after they shed their pollen. Usually the female flowers are produced singly or in pairs and their nut-like seeds arise from the top of a fleshy and swollen stalk (receptacle) that is red while the seeds remain green, even when ripe.

Hall's totara was named in honour of a Mr J.W. Hall, who lived in the southern Coromandel. It occurs in lowland, mountain and lower subalpine forests, from Northland to the southern North Island then throughout the South and Stewart Islands, except for the Canterbury Plains. Its timber is of very good quality but not quite as durable as that of the common totara. The bark can be peeled off and in earlier times was sometimes used as a roofing material for whares or huts. In coastal Southland and on Stewart Island it was formerly used to encase the inflated kelp bags that were used for storing and transporting the muttonbird harvest of the southern islands. The bark casing protected the bags from damage, during storage and transport, when the muttonbirds were traded with tribes from other districts. Such containers were known as pohatiti (titi being the name of the muttonbird).

Totara

The totara is a massive tree, one of the largest of our forest trees. It has a very large trunk that may be up to 30 m or more in height and up to 2 m, or even 3 m, or more in diameter. The trunk is clad with thick, fibrous, stringy, reddish-brown bark that is deeply furrowed and, on the lower portions of the trunk, it may be 7.5 cm or more thick. This thick, fibrous bark is particularly useful as an aid for identifying the tree.

Its leaves are rather similar to those of Hall's totara but may be slightly smaller. On young trees, especially those growing in more open situations, the crown is densely bushy, but on older trees it may be more open. The leaves vary from a dull brownish-green to a deep green and usually measure 1.5–3 cm long by about 3–4 mm wide. Usually they are straight to slightly curved and are sharply pointed. To the touch they can be quite prickly.

The strobili (pollen cones) are about 2 cm long and are produced either singly or in clusters of up to four together. The female flowers are either solitary or in pairs and the nut-like seeds sit on top of an orange or red, swollen and succulent receptacle (stalk). As with Hall's totara the seeds remain green, even when ripe. Flowering is generally during October or November and fruiting occurs in autumn. Tui often feed on the sweet fruit, and Maori once collected them for food.

Totara grows in lowland, lower mountain and lower subalpine forests throughout the North, South and Stewart Islands from about Mangonui in the far north southwards. It is one species that will regenerate quite readily.

Early Maori used the hard and durable totara timber in fire-making and for making their waka or canoes, especially the large war canoes, and it was particularly valued for carving. Maori custom demanded that whenever a totara was felled for timber, a young totara tree had to be planted to replace it so as to appease Tane, the god of the forest, for removing one of his children. Pakeha settlers also held totara timber in high regard and it was considered to be second only to kauri. Totara timber was used for bridge and wharf construction, railway sleepers, telegraph poles, as well as for general building purposes.

Miro

Miro is a handsome and fairly widespread tree that is easily recognised by its dark-coloured trunk, from which the bark falls off in thick, flat flakes. Its deep-green, slightly curved leaves are arranged along each side of the branchlets in two ranks or rows and they also serve to distinguish it. Miro is quite a large tree and will grow about 16–30 m tall, while its trunk may be up to about 1 m in diameter. When mature, its crown is densely bushy and has a round-headed appearance.

The leaves of juvenile miro trees are slightly longer than those of the adult and because no other native conifer has similar leaves even quite small juveniles are easily recognised. The leaves are 1.5–2.5 cm long by 2–3 mm wide, pointed at their tips, and on their undersurfaces the midrib is usually quite distinct.

The male strobili (pollen cones) are about 1.5 cm long and are produced from the leaf axils (between leaf and stem). The female flowers are solitary or occasionally paired and are produced on short branchlets. The sexes are on separate trees. The fleshy fruits are purplish-red and covered with a whitish, waxy bloom. They are about 2 cm long and slightly pointed at their tips. They may take more than 12 months to ripen, usually doing so during July–August. The fruits are a favourite food of the New Zealand pigeon, which will gorge themselves on them until they can hardly fly. The fruits have a turpentine-like flavour and when feeding on them the pigeons become very thirsty. Maori used to place water troughs in miro trees with snares set around their lips; when pigeons went to drink they were easily snared.

Miro timber is hard, straight-grained and beautifully figured. Although used for cabinetwork and turnery, its greatest use was for flooring. In Otago miro used to be referred to as black pine, which was confusing because *Prumnopitys taxifolia* is more commonly referred to by that name. In the East Cape district of the North Island its former Maori name was toromiro.

Miro is widespread in lowland forests throughout the North, South and Stewart Islands, except for the Canterbury Plains, and occurs to about 1000 m. It is quite common on the western side and in the southern portion of the South Island, and is a common tree of Stewart Island forests.

Matai

■ Juvenile has open, twiggy habit.

■ Adult bark is hammer-marked.

Height: 25 m

Scientific Name:
Prumnopitys taxifolia

While not dissimilar to miro, matai is quite easily distinguished. Firstly, juvenile matai trees go through a distinctive divaricating stage. They can usually be recognised when growing on the forest floor or in the understorey growth by their open, twiggy habit, flexuous branches and the sparseness of their usually brownish-coloured leaves as opposed to the deep green, denser leaves on adult trees. This juvenile phase was once regarded as being a separate species.

On adult trees the bark is an obvious means of identification. Generally, it has a hammer-marked appearance, the older bark falling off in smallish flakes and leaving small indentations. During the late winter and early spring trees become much more prone to shedding bark flakes and the newly exposed areas of bark are then distinctively reddish. The leaves of adult trees are arranged in two rows, and are 1–1.5 cm long by 1–2 mm wide, with the upper surfaces dark green and the undersides slightly glaucous (bluish-white). Male and female flowers are borne on separate trees. The male strobili (pollen cones) are on spikes of 10–30 cones per spike. This is also a point of difference because the miro strobili are produced only singly or at the most in pairs. Female flowers of matai are also produced on spikes about 4 cm long but with only 3–10 flowers per spike.

As with miro, the 1 cm-diameter round fruits take about 12 months to ripen, being almost black with a waxy bloom. They ripen March–April, and are eaten by New Zealand pigeons and kaka. Early Maori also ate the fruit, usually raw.

Miro timber was highly prized, being close-grained, heavy and of great strength and durability. Its colour varied from a light to a deep brown. It was used for construction purposes as well as railway sleepers and bridge piles, but it was greatly favoured for use as flooring, especially in public buildings.

Old matai trees may be up to 25 m tall and have a trunk that seldom exceeds 1 m in diameter. They usually have rounded crowns with erect branches. One very large tree, in South Westland, is estimated to be at least 1000 years old. Matai occurs throughout the North, South and Stewart Islands, except for the Canterbury Plains where it is rare. In colonial times it was commonly known as black pine.

Mountain toatoa

Generally, this species is smaller than its relatives, toatoa and tanekaha. It appears to exist as two distinct entities: one grows in lowland and montane forests and is a small tree, while the other largely occurs in mountain and subalpine regions where it is frequently no more than a bushy shrub.

The forest form usually occurs in low-altitude mountain forests in the central North Island and especially in lowland forests along the South Island west coast. In Southland it descends to sea level. The subalpine form occurs in the central North Island but is particularly common in the mountains of the South Island. The species is absent from the Canterbury Plains, Banks Peninsula, and North and Central Otago.

What appear to be the leaves of the three *Phyllocladus* species are in fact specialised flattened stems, known as phylloclades, that perform the functions of true leaves. These trees only ever have true leaves when they are small seedlings. One of the characteristics of mountain toatoa is that its phylloclades are distinctly aromatic when bruised or crushed. The thick, leathery phylloclades are variously shaped from roughly diamond-shaped to spoon-shaped, with their margins variously notched and lobed. Their characteristic celery-leaf shape means the tree is also known as mountain celery pine.

With the forest form of this species the phylloclades are usually up to 2.5 cm long, but on younger plants as well as some adult forms they may be quite a bit larger. The tree may grow to about 9 m tall with a trunk up to 30 cm wide, with bark that is usually a medium to light grey and with a somewhat warty or wrinkled appearance. The subalpine form is similar to the forest form except that it is usually smaller in all of its parts. Not infrequently, its phylloclades have a glaucous (whitish or greyish) hue.

One interesting feature of *Phyllocladus* is the way in which it produces its flowers. The male strobili (pollen cones) are produced from the tips of the branchlets, in clusters of 2–5 and, as they are often reddish to bright red, they are very noticeable. The inconspicuous female flowers arise during spring from along the margins of the phylloclades.

Toatoa is a particularly handsome tree that should easily be recognised because it is so distinct from its two relatives, the mountain toatoa and the tanekaha. In fact, one notable botanist once referred to it as 'the most charming of all the New Zealand pines'. It is confined to the northern half of the North Island but is inclined to be somewhat local in its distribution.

Toatoa will grow 6–15 m tall and may have a trunk up to 30–60 cm in diameter. As with the other species of *Phylloclladus* the bark has a somewhat warted appearance with short horizontal ridges running around it. The phylloclades (specialised flattened stems that perform the function of true leaves) are arranged, 10–20, along either side of a modified stem which gives the impression that it is the midrib of a normal leaf. They are more or less diamond-shaped and their undersurfaces are glaucous (whitish or greyish), especially when young, while the upper surfaces become bronze-coloured when mature. The phylloclades have a very thick and leathery texture and their margins are indented with small lobes or incisions. As with mountain toatoa and tanekaha, the only time toatoa has true leaves is when it a very small seedling; they then soon fall off as the phylloclades develop.

The male strobili (pollen cones) are produced in clusters of 10–20 at the tips of the branchlets. The female flowers are in rounded heads of 4–7 together, and arise near the bases of the modified stems during spring. *Phylloclladus toatoa* was formerly known as *P. glaucus* but under the rules of botanical nomenclature the name had to be changed and so the Maori name of toatoa was chosen as its new specific name. This species is more common in the far north, from Mangonui to Great Barrier Island, southwards to Cape Colville and then finally to a little to the south of Rotorua. It occurs in lowland to montane forests from sea level to about 600 m.

- ▮ Thick, leathery leaves (flattened stems); roughly diamond-shaped.
- ▮ Leaves bronzy when mature.

Height: 6–15 m

Scientific Name: *Phyllocladus toatoa*

- Leathery phylloclades (flattened stems) look like celery leaves.

- Foliage often symmetrical, with branchlets in regular tiers.

Height: 21 m

Scientific Name: *Phyllocladus trichomanoides*

Other Names: Celery pine, celery-topped pine

Tanekaha grows to a relatively large size and will attain heights of 21 m or more and its trunk may be up to 1 m in diameter. It can be a striking and beautiful tree.

The trunk has rather smooth, light-grey bark and is often attractively marked or patterned with the growth of lichens. Young trees have a distinctly pyramidal form and the branches are produced, from the trunk, in distinct whorls, but that is less obvious as the tree becomes older. The phylloclades (specialised flattened stems that perform the function of true leaves) are 1.2–2.5 cm long and are arranged, 10–15, along each side of a modified stem that varies from 2.5 to 7.5 cm long. As with the other species of *Phyllocladus* (mountain toatoa and toatoa), the only time that the tanekaha has true leaves is when it is quite a small seedling; they then soon fall off as the phylloclades develop. The phylloclades are irregularly diamond-shaped and have lobed and slightly incised margins.

The pollen catkins or strobili are 8–12 mm long, in clusters of 5–10. The female flowers are produced during spring in terminal clusters of 5–10 along the margins of modified phylloclades near the tips of the branchlets. The tanekaha occurs in lowland forests from North Cape southwards to about Wanganui in the west and Waipukurau in the east. Interestingly, along with one or two other North Island species, it then appears in the northern South Island, where it ranges from near Farewell Spit to near Westport, in south-western Nelson and then eastwards to the Marlborough Sounds.

Tanekaha wood is very straight-grained and has great strength. In early colonial times it was used for a variety of purposes including railway sleepers, pit props, marine work and some general construction. It is yellowish-white and has quite an elastic nature. The bark is rich in tannin and early Maori used to obtain a red dye from it. The tanekaha is also known as celery pine or celery-topped pine because the clusters of phylloclades, on its branchlets, resemble the foliage of a celery plant.

Pahautea

Small, scale-like leaves; branchlets only slightly flattened.

Mature trees have long, bare trunks and conical tops.

Height: 20–26 m

Scientific name: *Libocedrus bidwillii*

Other Names: Mountain cedar; (Maori) kaikawaka

Although pahautea has a rather close resemblance to kawaka or *Libocedrus plumosa*, the adult phase of the two can be readily distinguished. The branchlets of the former are more or less four-angled but slightly flattened, rather narrow, and 1.5 mm wide, while those of the latter are distinctly flattened and about 2 mm wide. The juvenile phase of pahautea also has flattened branchlets that are not always readily distinguished from those of kawaka, except that they are narrower.

Old, mature trees may be easily distinguished because of their cone-shaped appearance and because their deep-green foliage tends to form distinctive, billowing masses. Such older trees often stand out from among the surrounding trees because of their long, bare trunks and their conical tops. They may attain a height of 20–26 m. The leaves of juvenile trees are 3 mm long while those of adult trees are small and scale-like, being no more than 2 mm long.

The strobili (pollen cones) are about 7–11 mm long, borne singly at the tips of short branchlets, and are yellow when mature (see inset photo). The female cones are about 7–8 mm long and composed of four scales. When ripe they become quite woody and the scales begin to separate so that the seeds can be released.

Pahautea wood is red in colour, with a very straight grain. Its great durability meant it was formerly used for bridge construction, railway sleepers, house blocks, telegraph poles and roofing shingles. The species is often referred to simply as cedar but more commonly it is called mountain cedar or pahautea. Unfortunately, it is also referred to as kaikawaka, which is one of the names of *Libocedrus plumosa*, and this can be a source of confusion.

Pahautea is not uncommon in the wetter mountain forests and subalpine forests of the North Island from Mt Te Aroha southwards, while in the South Island it is most common on the western side of the main divide but is uncommon on the eastern side, occurring mainly on Banks Peninsula, the Otago Peninsula and in the Catlins area. In Westland it usually occurs from about 200 m above sea level and may ascend to an altitude of 800 m.

Kawaka

- Small, roughly triangular, scale-like leaves.
- Large trunk when mature, with stringy bark.

Height: 30 m

Scientific Name: *Libocedrus plumosa*

Other Names: (Maori) kaikawaka

Kawaka is a graceful and attractive tree that will grow to a height of 30 m and may have quite a large trunk from 60 cm to 1.2 m in diameter. Young plants have a rather narrow habit of growth and they can be distinguished from pahautea (*Libocedrus bidwillii*) by the branchlets being much wider, up to 7 mm. The branches of mature trees are wider-spreading, although the trees still retain a conical outline.

Kawaka bark is stringy and may fall away in quite long strips or ribbons. The branchlets of adult trees are narrower, about 3 mm wide and not quite so flattened. The triangular leaves are about 4 mm long and some project out from the sides of the branchlet, while those that are flattened along the upper and lower sides are no more than 1–2 mm long. The pollen cones or male strobili are 4–7 mm long and are produced from the tips of short branchlets. The female cones are about 1.2 cm long and are made up of four scales which, when ripe, become woody.

Kawaka wood is dark red with darker streaks, very strong and more durable than that of pahautea. It is easily split into very thin sections and because of that it was formerly used for roofing shingles. It was also used for general building purposes as well as posts and rails but was never common enough to be extensively used. In fact, it was more highly valued for cabinet and other ornamental work.

The kawaka is mainly a North Island species, occurring from Mangonui in the far north southwards to about Rotorua and northern Taranaki. From there it is not again seen until it reappears in the far north-west of the South Island from just south of Farewell Spit to West Wanganui Inlet and to just north of Takaka. It ranges from sea level to about 600 m. This species is also known as kaikawaka. It was originally collected by Robert Cunningham, in the Bay of Islands.

Kauri

- Conical when young.
- Tall, straight trunk.

Height: 30 m

Scientific Name: *Agathis australis*

Kauri may not be our tallest native tree but it is unquestionably the largest and noblest, and one of the most famous. A characteristic is that kauri trunks usually grow tall and straight, with very little taper, and they may be unbranched from 18–20 m or more. Such old, mature kauri trees are massive and unless one has actually seen one of the famous, ancient trees, such as Tane Mahuta in Waipoua Forest, it is difficult to comprehend their immensity.

On young kauri trees the bark is smooth and marked only by slightly raised scars (cicatrices) that partly encircle the trunk. On older trees the bark is smoother but characterised by thick, greyish flakes or scales that continually peel, thus preventing climbers and epiphytes from becoming established. On very old trees these shed flakes eventually form quite sizeable mounds around the base of the trunk. Bleeding gum is a common sight on the trunk.

The crown of a large kauri is quite enormous and wide-spreading, which makes the tree easy to identify, and it may support an array of perching plants. The trees reach to around 30 m high. Young trees (20–40 years or so), which are relatively fast-growing, have a completely different habit. They are pyramidal to almost columnar, with their uppermost branches tending to be erect, while those lower down are relatively short and more spreading.

The thick, leathery leaves of adult trees are up to 4 cm long, while those of juvenile trees may be larger and not as thick. While young trees are capable of producing strobili (pollen cones) from a fairly early age, generally they do not produce the larger female seed-bearing cones until they are about 40 years old. The female cones (pictured) are globular, 5–7.5 cm in diameter and, when ripe, their scales separate and fall away so as to release their seeds.

For Maori, kauri was favoured for making their large war canoes. Maori used the gum for chewing and in a tattooing pigment, and the gum also created a large industry in the colonial era, exported for use chiefly in varnish making. Kauri was also one of the most important of our timber trees, largely for ship building and house construction, with milling being so vast that the kauri forests were almost wiped out.

Kauri occurs in lowland and hilly forests from near North Cape to about Kawhia and the Bay of Plenty.

Taraire

- Large, leathery leaves, deep, shiny green.
- Velvety, rusty-brown hairs on branchlets, buds and young leaves.

Height: 20 m

Scientific Name: *Beilschmiedia tarairi*

This handsome tree is almost synonymous with the kauri forests of the north and can be one of the main components of the kauri forest, where it is a common understorey tree. It is easily recognised especially on account of its attractive foliage.

Taraire will grow to about 20 m tall and may have a large, spreading crown. The trunk is often very straight and may be up to 1 m in diameter. Apart from some pitting, its bark is dark brown and fairly smooth, which enables it to be easily recognised in the forest. Another distinguishing character that assists identification is its branchlets being densely clad with velvety, rusty-brown, fine hairs.

The large leaves are 7.5–15 cm long by 3.2–8.2 cm wide. They are rather thick and have a tough texture while their upper surfaces are deep green and shiny. The young leaves are also covered with rusty-brown hairs but they soon fall as the leaves mature. In spring taraire produces small, greenish flowers in panicles up to about 6.3 cm long. The flowers are followed in autumn by plum-like fruits that may be up to 3.5 cm long. When ripe they are a dark, blackish-purple and are readily consumed by New Zealand pigeons. Their turpentine taste makes them rather inedible. However, early Maori used to steam the kernels in an umu or earth oven for about two days to make them palatable.

Taraire wood is white with reddish heartwood and straight in the grain but was rather brittle and not greatly used, although it did lend itself to furniture making. Taraire grows in lowland and lower hill forests of the North Island from near North Cape to Raglan and the East Cape districts, but south of Auckland it is often local.

The tree was noted by Joseph Banks and Dr Daniel Solander in 1769 while on Captain Cook's first visit to New Zealand.

- Willow-like foliage.
- Smooth, black bark.

Height: 25 m

Scientific Name: *Beilschmiedia tawa*

Tawa is a fast-growing tree that may easily be recognised because of its willow-like foliage. It has an erect habit while the foliage hangs from the branchlets in a graceful manner. It makes quite a tall tree, up to 25 m or more, and its trunk can be up to 1.2 m in diameter. The bark is smooth and black. Older trees may be buttressed at the base.

Tawa leaves are 5–10 cm long by 1–3 cm wide, their tips are pointed and their bases taper to the petioles (stalks). Their upper surfaces are a light, yellowish-green while their undersurfaces are pale and almost whitish. The young leaves and branchlets are normally covered with fine, silky hairs. Small, greenish flowers are borne in panicles, up to about 8 cm long, that arise from the axils of the branchlets in late spring. The flowers are followed by quite large, dark purple, plum-like fruits (drupes), about 2.5 cm long, which normally ripen from late summer to early autumn (see lower photo). The fruits are eaten by New Zealand pigeons and kaka. Not infrequently the fallen fruits may be seen on the forest floor. As with taraire, the kernels of tawa fruits were cooked and eaten by Maori.

Tawa wood is white, very straight-grained and is easily split. In colonial times it was believed to have little value, but it was then discovered to be very useful for cooperage and dairy ware, particularly for butter kegs and boxes. Christchurch was the centre of this trade, the timber being obtained mainly from the Marlborough Sounds. Eventually, overcutting brought an end to such uses. Once cut for wood pulp, today tawa timber is used for flooring boards, for parquet flooring blocks and for plywood.

Early Maori used to manufacture their long bird spears from the straight-grained tawa. Both Maori and early European settlers used tawa for medicinal purposes. A decoction from the bark was used to cleanse wounds, while another decoction was used to relieve stomach aches and colds.

Tawa occurs in lowland and lower montane forests throughout the North Island, and in the northern part of the South Island from Nelson and the Marlborough Sounds southwards to about Westport and the Clarence River. It ascends to about 760 m.

Pigeonwood

Small to medium tree; deep-green, shiny leaves.

Leaves thick, leathery; distantly spaced teeth.

Height: 16 m

Scientific Name:
Hedycarya arborea

Other Names:
(Maori)
porokaiwhiri,
porokaiwhiriwhiri,
poporokaiwhiri

Pigeonwood becomes conspicuous in early summer when its scent fills the air and later when orange-red berries appear, the fruits being consumed in large quantities by the New Zealand pigeon, which gives the tree its common name. It is a small to medium tree, or occasionally only a tall shrub, and it occurs in lowland and montane forests throughout the North Island and in the warmer parts of the South Island to as far south as Banks Peninsula on the east coast and to northern Fiordland on the west. It will ascend from sea level to about 760 m. It also finds its northernmost limit on the Three Kings Islands.

Pigeonwood may grow to about 16 m tall and its trunk can be up to 50 cm in diameter. Its bark is quite dark to almost black and is quite smooth. The thick and leathery leaves are 5–12.5 cm long by 2–5 cm wide, their upper surfaces are deep green and shiny and they are somewhat paler beneath. Their margins have coarse and distantly spaced teeth, which usually makes the tree fairly easy to recognise. As occurs with many species of New Zealand trees, the pigeonwood's greenish male and female flowers are borne on separate trees. They are produced from the leaf axils in many-flowered, branched racemes, usually during October and November. The male flowers are about 8–12 mm in diameter while the female flowers are slightly smaller and they have a strong, aromatic scent. After flowering, the fruits develop on the female trees and when ripe (normally about October to February) they are bright orange to orange-red and about 1.5 cm long. At their tips they have a slight beak.

Pigeonwood timber was apparently never valued for any purpose. The tree is also known as porokaiwhiri, porokaiwhiriwhiri or poporokaiwhiri.

Pukatea

Pukatea is one of the taller forest trees, growing up to 36 m high. It frequently has a long, clean trunk and may have no branches for a considerable height. On large trees the trunk can be up to about 2 m in diameter. The pale bark is a light grey to almost whitish and that is often one character by which it may be recognised. It usually grows in damp or even wet places and another distinguishing character is its large, plank-like root buttresses which usually form at the base of its trunk. In some instances these buttresses may more than double the diameter of the trunk. Often quite large, old specimens may be seen left standing on farmland. Such trees usually regrow branches on the lower trunk so that its characteristic long, clean trunk is no longer obvious.

The branchlets are four-angled and, if examined closely, they are sparsely hairy when young, although the hairs soon fall off as the branchlet ages. The thick and leathery leaves are 4–7.5 cm long by 2.5–5 cm wide and their upper surfaces are deep green and glossy while the undersurfaces are paler. Their margins are coarsely and bluntly serrate (saw-like). Pukatea flowers are greenish-yellow, quite small and, interestingly, on the same tree they may be perfect (both male and female) or separately male and female. The flowers, usually from 6–9, may be produced on racemes up to 3 cm long that arise from the leaf axils. The fruits are not distinctly obvious. The green, jug-shaped seed cases release fluffy seeds in autumn.

Pukatea wood is pale brown in colour, cloudy and streaked with darker shades so that it can be quite ornamental. While it is rather soft it is very strong and tough, and does not easily split. Maori used it for carving, and in the colonial era it was used for boat building and sometimes as a cladding for building construction. Nowadays, it is not used at all.

The tree frequently occurs in wet forests where it most often grows along the banks of streams, in gullies and in swampy locations. It occurs in lowland districts throughout the North Island and in the South Island from Marlborough and Nelson southwards, down the western side of the island, to Fiordland. It ascends from sea level to about 600 m.

Mahoewao

- Bright green, willow-like leaves, finely toothed.

- Conspicuous blue-black berries in March–April.

Height: 6 m

Scientific Name:
Melicytus lanceolatus

Other Names:
(Maori) kaiweta

Mahoewao is quite a small tree, reaching around 6 m high, which, when growing in forest, has a rather erect, branching habit, but in open situations it may be more widely spreading and has quite a dense, bushy top. It may easily be recognised by its bright green leaves being willow-like, except that they are finely toothed around their margins.

The trunk of the mahoewao may be up to 30 cm in diameter and its slightly roughened bark is normally a whitish colour. Its leaves are usually 7.5–15 cm long by 4 mm–3 cm wide. In common with other members of the genus, the male and female flowers are produced on separate trees. It is also of interest to note that, botanically, it belongs to the violet family (Violaceae), even though its flowers do not remotely resemble those of the violet, so familiar to gardeners and florists. The small, yellowish flowers are in clusters of 2–6 that are produced in spring from the leaf axils on the upper part of the branchlet or even lower down from the bare branchlet itself. Sometimes, the small petals of the flowers may be purplish in colour. The berries are about 7 mm long and, although small, they are usually in such quantity that they are quite conspicuous. They generally ripen during March and April and are blue-black or dark purple in colour.

Mahoewao is a not uncommon component of lowland to montane forests, and often forest margins, in the North, South and Stewart Islands from about Kaitaia southwards. In the South Island it is more common west of the main divide and is generally absent from southern Marlborough, Canterbury, North and Central Otago. It then reappears about Dunedin and is present around the southern coastal area of Southland. It occurs from sea level to about 900 m. Mahoewao is also sometimes known as kaiweta.

Mahoe / Whiteywood

- Whitish bark.
- Profuse purple-black berries.

Height: 10 m

Scientific Name:
Melicytus ramiflorus

Other Names:
(Maori)
hinahina
(South Is.)

Mahoe is a common tree over most of New Zealand except for the Canterbury Plains, the southern part of Southland and Stewart Island. In these two latter areas its place is taken by mahoewao. It grows in lowland and montane forests from sea level to about 900 m. It is also a common component of the scrublands that regenerate after forest has been cleared.

Mahoe was originally collected by Joseph Banks and Dr Daniel Solander who accompanied Captain Cook on his first voyage to New Zealand in 1769. It is not a large tree and seldom grows to more than 10 m tall; usually it has a spreading habit and its trunk may be 30–50 cm in diameter. The bark is frequently a distinctive whitish colour, hence its common name of whiteywood.

The bright green leaves are 5–15 cm long by 3–5 cm wide and they have rather coarsely toothed margins. The greenish to yellowish flowers appearing in early summer are quite small, about 3–4 mm in diameter, and they are produced in clusters of 2–10 from the leaf axils along the upper part of the branchlet while, at the same time, numerous clusters of flowers also appear from the bare, older branchlets. In fact, its specific name of *ramiflorus* means to flower on the older branches and refers to that habit. The berries, about 5 mm in diameter, may vary from a lovely violet to such a dark purple that they appear to be almost black. The fruits usually ripen during February and March, and in a good season will cover the branchlets very profusely. They provide food for native birds, including tui, silvereyes and whiteheads.

Mahoe wood is very brittle and had no value as a timber, but its foliage is very palatable to farm stock so that during dry seasons farmers would cut off branches for use as cattle fodder. Early Maori used mahoe wood for generating fire by friction. A small flat block of mahoe wood would be rubbed with a pointed stick of kaikomako so that the hard kaikomako stick would wear a groove in the soft mahoe wood. After some time a little ball of fluff would gather at one end of the groove and, by blowing on it, it could be induced to burst into flame. In the south of the South Island mahoe is known as hinahina.

Tree fuchsia / Kotukutuku

- Light-brown, papery, peeling bark.
- Gnarled, twisted branches.

Height: 12 m

Scientific name: *Fuchsia excorticata*

Other Names: Fuchsia; (Maori) konini (Westland), kohutuhutu

Tree fuchsia is the largest species of fuchsia, a genus that extends to Tahiti, and then from Mexico to southern South America. It will grow to about 12 m or more tall and is usually rather wide-spreading. The tree is easily recognised by its light-brown bark that peels off the trunk and main branches. As the bark peels it exposes even paler young bark from underneath; generations of young boys have used this papery bark as a substitute for tobacco. Generally, the trunk and main branches have a rather twisted and gnarled form which further aids identification. Particularly in southern forests, some massive, old specimens can be seen.

The soft leaves are 5–10 cm long by 2.5–5 cm wide, their upper surfaces deep green and the undersurfaces silvery. The flowers produced in late spring are 2–3.2 cm long and pendent, on long, slender stalks that may be up to 1.5 cm long. When the flowers first open they are green with purplish shades but as they age they become purplish and, finally, quite a deep red. The pollen of the tree fuchsia is blue, a rare colour for any flower. The flowers are followed in summer by succulent purple to blackish berries that are about 1.5 cm long. These berries are known as konini and, especially in Westland, the whole tree is known as the konini tree. In some districts jam used to made from these berries. Nectar-eating birds such as the silvereyes, tui and bellbirds delight in the flowers, as they do with the berries, which quickly disappear when ripe. New Zealand pigeons and whiteheads also enjoy the fruit.

Very strong and hard, fuchsia wood is also very ornamental, being deep brown with broad, paler streaks as well as black markings. It has been used for making ornamental brooches, for wood turning and inlay work. The wood is difficult to burn so old bushmen used to refer to it as 'bucket-of-water wood'.

Tree fuchsia is common in lowland and lower montane forests throughout the North, South and Stewart Islands, except for the Canterbury Plains, and it ranges from sea level to 1060 m. Although most commonly known as fuchsia or tree fuchsia, it is also called kotukutuku and kohutuhutu. In the colder districts (especially in mountain areas) it is usually deciduous and the leaves may turn a buttery-yellow in the autumn before they fall.

Toru

Long, narrow, thick, leathery leaves.

Old leaves can turn bright red.

Height: 12 m

Scientific Name: *Toronia toru*

Toru is a most handsome tree that is quite easily recognised by its long, narrow, thick and leathery leaves. Not infrequently, the old leaves turn a bright red as they die which is another character that aids recognition. Old trees can be up to 12 m or more in height and have a trunk 30–60 cm in diameter. Its usually erect growth is much-branched, mostly from the base, and it does not have much of a trunk.

The leaves are 10–20 cm long by 8–16 mm wide, and their upper surfaces are deep green and shiny while their apexes (tips) are pointed. Toru flowers usually appear during October–November and are produced on erect, 6–16-flowered racemes that are about 5 cm long. The individual yellowish flowers have four petals and are sweetly scented with a honey-like fragrance. The opened flowers contrast quite prettily with the rusty-brown of the unopened buds. The flowers are followed by a fruit that is about 1.2–1.8 cm long, which becomes a reddish colour as it ripens. Inside its fleshy coat it has a single stone or seed.

Toru wood is a deep-red colour but because it was never available in quantity or of a sufficient size it had no commercial value; however, it was once used for inlay work by cabinetmakers.

Toru occurs in lowland to montane scrublands and forests from Mangonui, in the far north, southwards to Rotorua and Tokomaru Bay in the East Cape district. In a number of areas it is rare and local apart from habitats such as the gumlands of Northland where it may be more common. It ascends from sea level to about 850 m.

Rewarewa

- **Leathery leaves coarsely toothed.**
- **Partly coiled, dark-red flowers.**

Height: 30 m

Scientific name: *Knightia excelsa*

Other Names: New Zealand honeysuckle

Of the forest trees, rewarewa is one of the most striking because of its lofty and rather erect habit of growth. In general appearance it can be likened to a Lombardy poplar and can easily be recognised when it towers above the lower forest. It will attain heights of up to 30 m and its trunk may be up to a metre or more in diameter. The bark is greyish, dark brown or almost black and has a very finely warted texture.

The very tough and leathery leaves are one of the species' distinguishing characteristics. On young trees they can be 10–25 cm long by 2–3 cm wide, while those of an adult tree are 10–15 cm or more long by 2.5–4 cm wide. The leaves are very rigid with a very hard texture and their margins, which are coarsely toothed, may be rather undulating. The young shoots and the undersurfaces of the leaves are clad with a fine tomentum of dark, rusty-brown hairs.

One of the most interesting things about the rewarewa is its flowers. In late spring they are produced in dense racemes about 10 cm long that arise either singly or in pairs from the axils of the leaves and from bare parts of the branchlets. Each raceme has about 50–80 flowers, on short stalks; the individual flowers are about 4 cm long. The dark-red flowers have four parts or corolla lobes and, as the flower buds open, the individual lobes separate and coil tightly outwards to form a tangled mass around the bases of the flowers. The pistils are then left with their club-shaped tips (the female part of the flower) projecting outwards like the bristles of a bottlebrush. Rewarewa is largely pollinated by birds, such as tui, bellbirds and silvereyes, which seek the nectar from its flowers. (Maori also once collected the nectar, and today rewarewa honey is popular.) The seeds are produced in woody capsules that take nearly 12 months to ripen, and when they open, to release the seeds, they resemble a miniature boat.

Rewarewa wood is very ornamental, being figured with darker mottling on a pale or reddish ground. However, it has never been widely used, apart from fine furniture and inlay work.

Rewarewa grows in lowland and montane forests throughout the North Island, and in the South Island in the Marlborough Sounds area and on D'Urville Island.

Tree tutu

■ **Common in regenerating areas.**

■ **Leaves distinctly veined, paired on thin stems.**

Height: 8 m

Scientific Name:
Coriaria arborea

Other Names:
(Maori) tutu

Tree tutu is probably best known because of its poisonous qualities and, although most people do not consider it as such, it is actually a very handsome and striking plant that should not fail to attract attention. It is probably because most people are familiar with its poisonous nature that they tend to disregard any other qualities it may have.

The poisonous principal of tutu is a substance known as tutin, the young stems containing more tutin than the old stems, and the leaves of tree tutu contain more tutin than the stems of any other native species of *Coriaria*. Most cases of poisoning from tutu seem to occur with stock browsing on the plant and, apart from the very early days, there do not appear to be any more recent cases of people suffering from tutu poisoning.

It is a widely spread small tree that occurs in most parts of New Zealand and, after land disturbance or clearance, such as when slips occur, it is one of the first colonising plants to appear.

Tree tutu will grow to about 8 m in height and usually has a very short trunk that may be up to 30 cm in diameter. Generally, it has mainly multiple trunks arising from or near to ground level. Its bark is dark brown or greyish and on old trees is usually furrowed. The stems of younger plants are fluted and marked with rather conspicuous lenticels. Its handsome leaves are 5–8 cm or more long by 4–5 cm wide and are usually paired along thin stems. Their upper surfaces are deep green and shiny and they are distinctly veined. The very small, greenish flowers are produced on racemes that are from 15–20 cm long and generally hang downwards. Flowering generally occurs from October to about December but may continue until later. The fruits are about 4 mm in diameter, quite succulent, dark, shiny purple, about 4 mm long and they may ripen between November and April.

Tree tutu occurs throughout the North, South, Stewart and Chatham Islands, except for the Canterbury Plains, in scrublands, around forest margins and along roadsides. It commonly occurs on alluvial ground from sea level to about 1060 m. The vigorous young shoots that grow from the base of the tree during spring have been likened in appearance to giant shoots of asparagus.

Karo

- Leaves have whitish/pale-buff hairs beneath.
- Black seeds in sticky orange secretion in opened capsule.

Height: 9 m

Scientific Name:
Pittosporum crassifolium

Commonly known as karo, this is an easily recognised small tree particularly because of its quite large and conspicuous seed capsules and also its leaves that are thickly clad with a felted mass of fine, whitish or pale-buff hairs on their undersurfaces. Karo is strictly a coastal tree from the upper half of the North Island where it occurs mainly from North Cape to about Poverty Bay on the east coast. Because of cultivation, karo has spread far beyond its natural range and now occurs as far south as Wellington. It was once thought to also occur on the Kermadec Islands but it is now considered that the Kermadec plant is a different species.

Karo will grow to about 9 m tall and generally has rather erect growth. Its bark is grey or dark brown to blackish, while the young branchlets, leaf stalks, undersides of the leaves and immature fruits are covered with downy hairs. The dark-green leaves are 5–7.5 cm long by 2–2.5 cm wide and have shiny upper surfaces. Although small, the heavily scented flowers of karo are relatively conspicuous. They are bright to dark red and are produced in 5–10-flowered umbels, in September–October. The flowers are followed by seed capsules, maturing the following February, that may be up to 3 cm in diameter and they usually have three to four valves. When the capsules ripen and burst open they are equally conspicuous because the thick and woody valves open widely to display a whitish interior upon which sit a number of shiny black seeds partially immersed in a sticky, orange secretion. Birds enjoy these seeds, as they do the nectar.

Karo occurs mainly along streamsides and around forest margins, generally not too far from the coast, and it ranges from sea level to about 950 m. It is particularly adapted for growth in coastal areas and, as well as resisting ferocious salt-laden gales, it even grows in places where it has to endure the influence of wind-blown sea spray.

Lemonwood / Tarata

- Sweetly scented greenish-yellow flowers.
- Crushed leaves have lemony scent.

Height: 12 m

Scientific Name:
Pittosporum eugenioides

Lemonwood is one of the commonest of New Zealand's small trees, occurring throughout both the North and South Islands but absent from Stewart Island. In the South Island, apart from Riccarton Bush at Christchurch, it does not occur on the Canterbury Plains but it can be found on the Canterbury foothills.

It will attain a height of up to 12 m and may have quite a substantial trunk that can be up to 60 cm or more in diameter. The bark of the trunk and main stems is generally whitish, or pale grey on the oldest parts of the tree, but is fairly smooth on the younger branches. The bark can be quite resinous and produces a whitish gum.

The leaves are quite distinct from those of other species of *Pittosporum*. They are alternate to more or less whorled, 5–12.5 cm long by 2.5–4 cm wide, and they have entire margins that are more or less undulating. Their shiny upper surfaces are a very attractive medium green to yellowish-green and they are also distinguished by their midribs being conspicuously whitish or pale cream.

Flowering usually occurs between October and December, the flowers being produced in terminal clusters. They are a very attractive greenish-yellow or yellowish-cream colour, about 1–1.5 cm in diameter, and are very sweetly scented with a honey-like fragrance but, in excess, the scent can be quite overpowering. The egg-shaped seed capsules are about 7 mm long, and are green at first but become almost black when ripe. They normally take around 12 months or so to ripen so that it is possible to see the ripe seed capsules on the tree at the same time that it flowers.

Lemonwood occurs in lowland to montane forests, especially along the banks of creeks and the margins of forest from sea level to 760 m. It is also commonly known as tarata and in the past has also had a number of other common names. Its common European name derives from the fact that its crushed leaves give off a lemon-like smell. Its wood is white, very tough and elastic, but has never had any economic use. Early Maori used the resin from the bark to perfume oil, while the leaves and flowers were crushed or bruised and mixed with fat as an ointment to anoint their bodies.

Pittosporum ralphii

■ Large, thin leaves, dull deep green.

■ Reddish flowers from tips of branchlets.

Height: 4–6 m

While *Pittosporum ralphii* is closely related to karo or P. *crassi-folium*, it may be readily recognised by its larger, thinner leaves that are oblong and suddenly narrow to a distinct petiole (stalk) without the base gradually narrowing as do those of karo. *Pittosporum ralphii* is a small tree about 4–6 m tall and its trunk may be up to 45 cm or more in diameter. It has dark-brown or greyish bark which is usually rather smooth. When growing in a more open situation, its crown is quite widely spreading.

The leaves of P. *ralphii* are 5–12.5 cm long by 2.5–5 cm wide. Their upper surfaces are deep green and rather dull, or with a slight sheen, while their undersurfaces are thinly clad with a whitish or buff tomentum. The leaf margins are flat to somewhat recurved and they are also sometimes slightly undulating.

The flowers are reddish and are in 3–10-flowered umbels, produced from the tips of the branchlets. Flowering usually occurs between September and December. Its seed capsules are similar to those of P. *crassifolium*, but slightly smaller, being about 1.5 cm long. The seed capsules normally do not ripen until November or January. They are three-valved and when ripe split wide open. Inside them sit numerous shiny, black seeds that are held by a sticky, orange secretion.

P. *ralphii* is distributed throughout the central North Island from the Thames district southwards to about Wanganui in the west and Dannevirke in the east. Normally, the tree grows around forest margins and along streamsides in scrubby country and is frequent in the Hawke's Bay district.

This species was named after a Dr Ralph of Patea, who presumably discovered it, but it has never had a common name.

Kohuhu

Pittosporum tenuifolium is a very variable small tree that exists in a number of forms. It will sometimes grow to 10–15 m tall and in more open situations forms a round-headed tree. Usually its trunk is 30–40 cm in diameter.

It comprises two subspecies, both commonly known as kohuhu: subspecies *tenuifolium* and subspecies *colensoi*. Superficially they are quite similar but differ in their distribution. Subspecies *tenuifolium* occurs throughout the North Island and in the South Island east of the main divide, whereas subspecies *colensoi* occurs in the North Island southwards from about Kawhia and the Bay of Plenty, and in the South Island mainly west of the main divide. Both subspecies tend to meet in the Invercargill area.

Subspecies *colensoi* is often a slightly larger tree and has larger leaves with margins that are not so distinctly undulating as those of subspecies *tenuifolium*.

On both subspecies the bark is dark brown to almost black and usually has a slightly roughened surface, hence the common name of black mapou that was once used. The leaves of subspecies *tenuifolium* are 2.5–6 cm long by 1.6–2.5 cm wide. Their upper surfaces are usually bright to deep green and shiny with the margins barely to quite strongly undulating. Those of subspecies *colensoi* are 5–10 cm long by 2–5 cm wide, dark green and shiny above and with flat to slightly undulating margins. The flowers of both are dark reddish-purple to almost black and are produced singly from the leaf axils or in small clusters, usually in October–November. They are sweetly scented, particularly in the evening, as that helps to attract the night-flying insects that pollinate them. Their seed capsules, about 12 mm in diameter, become quite woody when ripe. As with other species of *Pittosporum* the shiny, black seeds are embedded in a sticky secretion. They generally ripen from January to March.

The white-coloured wood was never available in sufficient quantity for economic use, although it is very strong. Maori once collected the gum to scent hair and use in medicines. For many years this species was erroneously known as matipo, which is a corruption of matipou, a name that should more correctly be applied to *Myrsine australis*. In colonial days it was also confusingly known by other common names such as black mapou, black maple and tawhiwhi.

Kanuka

■ Foliage softer, finer than manuka.

■ Flowers smaller than manuka; occur in clusters.

Height: 15 m

Scientific Name: *Kunzea ericoides*

Other Names: Tea tree, white tea tree; (Maori) manuka (Northland)

Ever since the early days there has always been confusion between kanuka and manuka (*Leptospermum scoparium*); the old bushmen often did not differentiate between the two species. In Northland *Kunzea ericoides* is known as manuka, which does not help the situation one bit, while both *K. ericoides* and *L. scoparium* are also indiscriminately, commonly known as tea tree. To add to the confusion, both species were originally classified under *Leptospermum*, until 1983, when *L. ericoides* was placed in the large Australian genus of *Kunzea*.

No matter what it is called, kanuka is a handsome small tree that will grow to 15 m or more tall and may have a trunk 30–90 cm in diameter. Its rather papery bark peels off in long, narrow strips.

Although there is some resemblance between kanuka and manuka, the former may be recognised by its softer and finer foliage that is either alternate or produced in small clusters. Its leaves are 4–12 mm long by 1–2 mm wide and do not have pointed tips as in manuka. A further difference is that the white kanuka flowers are usually smaller than those of manuka, being 3–7 mm wide. The flowers are aromatic but not strongly scented, and are generally produced in clusters of 2–5 flowers but not singly as in manuka. In most seasons, kanuka flowers will smother the tree in great profusion. The seed capsules are from 2–4 mm in diameter (narrower and longer than manuka capsules).

Kanuka occurs throughout the North Island in lowland to montane scrublands and often forms thickets and transition forests (which will eventually regenerate into mixed forest), especially on land that has formerly been forested. In the South Island it occurs from Nelson southwards to the Buller River, throughout Marlborough and down the eastern side of the main divide to about the Clutha River. It is absent from most of Westland, all of Fiordland and Southland. It was formerly common on the Canterbury Plains but is now restricted to a small area on the northern plains. Kanuka ascends to about 900 m.

Its red-coloured wood is very hard and nowadays is mainly used for firewood. In former times it was used by Maori for manufacturing weapons, while European settlers used it for jetty piles, wheel spokes, tool handles and fencing.

Manuka

- Stiff, sharply pointed leaves.
- White, sometimes pink, flowers occur singly.

Height: 1–10 m

Scientific Name: *Leptospermum scoparium*

Other Names: Tea tree

Manuka is a small tree that occurs virtually over all of New Zealand, in all manner of situations, from the Three Kings Islands to Stewart Island and the subantarctic Snares Islands. It extends from sea level to about 1370 m.

Depending upon its habitat it may vary from a tree up to about 10 m tall to a dwarf mountain shrub less than 1 m high. It is similar to kanuka but differs in having sharply pointed leaves and in its flowers being produced singly from the leaf axils. Another distinguishing character is its bark which, on old trees, is shed in long strips or ribbons. The bark can often have a sooty colouring, as a result of the sooty mould fungus growing on the honeydew secretions of the manuka blight. The trunk can be up to 60 cm in diameter, rarely larger.

Manuka branchlets are covered with silky, whitish hairs. The small leaves are 4–10 mm long by 2–6 mm wide and, unlike kanuka, they are hard to the touch. The distinctly honey-scented flowers are produced either from the leaf axils or on short branchlets. They are up to 1.6 cm (or more on varieties from the far north) wide and are mainly white, but it is not uncommon to find plants on which the flowers are flushed with pink. In the far north there is a variety (*incanum*) with much larger flowers that are distinctly pink-coloured. Flowering is from early November until late January, but in warmer parts of the country it is not unusual to come across plants with some flowers on them all year round, even during winter. The woody seed capsules are top-shaped and are about 7–14 mm in diameter (broader than kanuka).

Manuka wood is red-coloured, very hard and durable. Once used for tool handles and fencing, these days it is not much used, apart from firewood, and sawdust for smoking fish. The first European use of manuka was when Captain James Cook visited in 1773 and brewed it into a tea-like drink that the crew drank for the prevention of scurvy. The early settlers also used manuka as a substitute for tea, hence its common name of tea tree. The first recorded use of this name occurred in 1834. The leaves of manuka contain a fragrant oil that has beneficial properties and its flowers provide an excellent honey.

Ramarama

- Leaves blistered or puckered.
- Creamy-white flowers in summer.

Height: 6 m

Scientific Name: *Lophomyrtus bullata*

Ramarama is a small forest tree that will grow to about 6 m or so tall and generally does not have a wide-spreading habit. It is easily recognised by its leaves being quite distinct from that of any other native tree. They have a very blistered, or puckered, appearance. It occurs in coastal and lowland forests, often preferring the more open parts, especially around forest margins and in clearings. Ramarama is found throughout much of the North Island and in the South Island in the northern Nelson and Marlborough regions. It ranges from sea level to 600 m.

The rather smooth bark is mid-brownish in colour. The leaves are 2.5–5 cm long by 2–3 cm wide, arranged oppositely, and apart from their blistered appearance they are usually characterised by being a reddish colour, especially if growing in a more open situation. The leaves of trees growing in shadier parts of the forest generally do not have that reddish colour but instead are medium green to a light yellowish-green. The flowers are produced singly from the leaf axils, on slender stalks and they are usually 1–2 cm in diameter. They are, generally, a creamy-white but sometimes may have a rosy flush. Usually the tree flowers during December and January. Its fruits are about 1 cm long and are a dark reddish-purple, becoming almost black when ripe.

Ramarama wood is red and straight-grained, and is very strong and tough. It was never readily available, except in small quantities, but was sometimes used for tool handles or for ornamental purposes, especially inlay work.

Rohutu

- Smooth, slightly peeling bark.
- Small, heart-shaped leaves.

Height: 6 m

Scientific Name:
Lophomyrtus obcordata

Rohutu is a small tree that can easily be recognised by its smooth, slightly peeling bark; in fact one of its greatest attributes is its lovely trunk, showing attractive patterns of new and old bark (see inset photo). The new bark is pale and greenish-white while the old bark is a light, almost cinnamon colour. The trunk of an old tree may be up to 30 cm in diameter. Rohutu will grow to about 6 m tall and, if in an open situation, will have quite a bushy crown, but if in a shadier place its growth will tend to be more erect.

Its leaves are of an inverted heart shape, being broadest towards their slightly notched tips. They are 5–12 mm long and arranged in opposite pairs or clusters. The undersurfaces of the leaves are conspicuously dotted with small oil glands. As with ramarama, the creamy-white flowers are produced singly from the leaf axils and are about 7 mm in diameter, and they have four rounded petals. Flowering generally occurs during December and January. The berries of rohutu are similar to those of ramarama, being about 7 mm long, and their colour varies from bright to dark red, or to a dark violet that is almost black.

Rohutu occurs in coastal and hilly forests throughout the North Island from about Ahipara southwards, and throughout the South Island except for the Canterbury Plains; it is absent from much of Southland. Its uses were similar to those of ramarama, such as in tool handles or for ornamental purposes, and like that species, the wood was never available in sufficient quantity to allow it to be much used.

Pohutukawa

■ Leathery, shiny deep-green leaves.

■ Crimson flowers from early summer.

Height: 20 m

Scientific Name: *Metrosideros excelsa*

Other Names: Christmas tree, New Zealand Christmas tree

Pohutukawa is one of the best known and loved of our native trees, as well as being one of the most spectacular, its crimson blooms from early summer earning it the name of Christmas tree or New Zealand Christmas tree.

In its natural range pohutukawa grows around coastal areas and in coastal forests in the North Island from Cape Reinga to Poverty Bay on the east coast and to Urenui in north Taranaki on the west coast. It also occurs around the shore and islets of Lake Taupo and other central North Island lakes. So successfully has it been planted around southern North Island coastal areas that most people believe it is also native to those areas. It has also been planted extensively around warmer South Island coastlines.

The pohutukawa is quite a large tree with a very spreading habit of growth, its lower branches growing out more or less horizontally, for considerable distances, from its short and gnarled trunk. It will grow to 20 m or more in height and may have a spread of 38 m or more. The trunk may be 60 cm–1.8 m in diameter and it often branches into several main stems. Its fissured bark is greyish, thick and stringy and usually peels off in long strips. A feature of old pohutukawa trees can be the large beard-like masses of aerial roots that grow out from some of the lower branches.

On seedlings the leaves are quite smooth and hairless but after 4–5 years they begin to assume their adult foliage, which is thick and leathery with deep-green, shiny upper surfaces and undersurfaces covered with a dense, white, felted tomentum. The leaves, in pairs, are 2.5–10 cm long by 1.5–5 cm wide. The flowers vary in colour but are generally a bright to deep crimson. Some flowering starts in November but the main period is December to mid-January. The flowers are in clusters and, while individual flowers have red petals, the petals are small and generally hidden by the numerous stamens of each flower.

The large quantities of nectar provide honey for apiarists and is greatly favoured by various native birds, including tui and bellbirds. It has also been discovered that some species of native gecko pollinate the flowers when they feed on the nectar, during the evenings. Pohutukawa wood is very strong and its gnarled and bent branches were used for boat building.

Rata

■ Leathery leaves have blunt tips.

■ Flowers dull to bright red.

Height: 20–30 m

Scientific Name: *Metrosideros robusta*

Other Names: Northern rata

Rata is one of the largest of our native trees, attaining heights of 20–30 m, while its trunk may be 1–3.5 m in diameter. As well as having an exceptionally large trunk it also has a massive, spreading crown, usually home to many perching plants. It is very floriferous and a rata tree in full bloom is a fitting rival to the pohutukawa.

Contrary to popular belief, the rata frequently, but by no means invariably, commences life as an epiphytic seedling that has germinated high up in the crown of one of the large forest trees such as rimu. Once it attains a reasonable size it will send out roots that travel down its host's trunk until they reach the ground. At that stage the growth of the rata will then accelerate. If several roots grow down to the ground, they may coalesce and appear as if they are strangling the host tree. Not all rata trees commence life as epiphytes, however, and some (especially in the South Island) may begin life as a normal tree in the ground.

Rata bark is thin and falls away in small, rectangular flakes. Its quite thick and leathery leaves are 2.5–5 cm long by 1.5–2 cm wide. Their blunt tips distinguish them from those of the closely related *Metrosideros umbellata*, the leaves of which are sharply pointed. The upper surfaces of rata leaves are deep green with a slight sheen and the numerous translucent oil glands with which they are dotted can be seen when the leaves are held up to the light. The flowers are somewhat variable in colour, from a dull red to a brilliant, vibrant red and they are produced in terminal clusters. Nectar is collected by native birds, including kaka, tui and bellbirds.

Rata is abundant in coastal, lowland and hilly forests throughout the North Island and on the western side of the South Island from western Nelson to just north of Greymouth. It ascends from sea level to about 900 m. Rata wood is extremely hard and dense, and it was used for a variety of purposes, including ships' timbers, tramway sleepers, the heavy framework of railway wagons, bridges, wharves and other construction work. Rata is also known as northern rata in order to distinguish it from southern rata (M. *umbellata*), regardless of the fact that both species occur in both the North and South Islands.

Southern rata

- **Leathery leaves have sharply pointed tips.**
- **Brilliant red flowers.**

Height: 10–20 m

Scientific Name: *Metrosideros umbellata*

Other Names: (Maori) rata

In spite of being known commonly as southern rata, this species occurs throughout much of the North Island as well as the South and Stewart Islands and on the subantarctic Auckland Islands.

It is easily distinguished from rata (M. *robusta*) by its thick, leathery leaves which are 4–7.5 cm long by 1–2 cm wide with sharply pointed tips and shiny upper surfaces. Their paler undersurfaces are dotted with numerous small oil glands. Southern rata forms a tree 10–20 m tall and generally has a much-branched crown, often host to perching plants. Its trunk may be up to 1 m or more in diameter and has papery, brown to greyish bark that peels off in small flakes. The brilliant red flowers are produced in clusters from the tips of short branchlets and they are more vibrant than those of M. *robusta*. Depending on locality, flowering may commence in November and at higher altitudes continue until March. Frequently, the southern rata does not flower well every year and good flowering seasons may occur only every three or four years. When it does have a good season, whole mountainsides will be aflame with the brilliancy of its flowers. Many native birds, including kea, feed on the nectar.

Southern rata wood is very hard and dense and thus it was formerly known as iron-wood. It has been used for boat building.

Southern rata occurs in lowland to montane forests and scrubland, or even in subalpine forests, in the North Island from near Kaitaia to the Tararua Range, but it may be rare and local. In the South Island it is common, particularly in Westland and Fiordland, and less so to the east of the main divide. It is also common on Stewart Island and on the subantarctic Auckland Islands where it forms quite dense forests. It extends from sea level to about 760 m. In Southland some very old trees have obviously fallen over into a reclining position and from them new trunks have grown up to form more erect trees. From their size, it is estimated that these later erect growths would probably be several hundred years old. Well-known sites for the southern rata, when the season is conducive to a good display, are the Otira Gorge and the Haast River Valley. Southern rata is usually terrestrial and seldom, if ever, commences life as an epiphyte as does M. *robusta*.

Whau

- Small tree with large, soft leaves.
- Spiny seed capsules.

Height:
6–7 m

Scientific Name:
Entelea arborescens

Other Names:
(Maori) hauama

Whau is a small tree of tropical appearance and is easily recognised. Its large, soft leaves and bristly or spiny seed capsules are often sufficient to identify it. It will grow to a height of about 6–7 m, but in more exposed situations may be no more than a shrub.

Whau occurs in coastal forests but is not a particularly common tree and has a rather localised distribution. It is more common in the northern part of the North Island from near Cape Reinga to about as far south as the Mokau River in Taranaki, the Bay of Plenty and along the East Cape coast to Hawke Bay. South of those areas it is localised in the more southern part of the North Island. It is also common on some of the offshore islands such as the Three Kings and Mayor Island. In the South Island it occurs near the base of Farewell Spit, around the shores of Golden Bay, Tasman Bay and in the Marlborough Sounds. On the mainland whau usually grows in sheltered gullies and along the bases of cliffs, although in some localities it may grow in more exposed situations. It ascends from sea level to about 200 m.

The trunk may be up to 25 cm in diameter. While the bark has a more or less smooth appearance, it is generally roughened or pitted with lenticels and old leaf scars. The leaves of a well-grown plant can be very large. They are on long petioles (stalks) that may be up to 60 cm in length and the leaf-blade is 15–25 cm long by 15–20 cm wide. The blade is sharply pointed, the margins are sharply toothed and the base, where it joins the leaf petiole, is heart-shaped. It has quite large, white flowers, about 2–2.5 cm in diameter, which have numerous golden stamens in their centres and are produced in large clusters. After flowering the distinctive seed capsules develop. They are rigidly spiny or bristly and at first are green but as they ripen change to a brown or brownish-grey colour. Flowering is generally October–January.

Whau wood has the reputation of being one of the lightest known, and it is said to be about half of the weight of cork. It was used by Maori to make floats for fishing nets. The tree is also known as hauama.

Wineberry

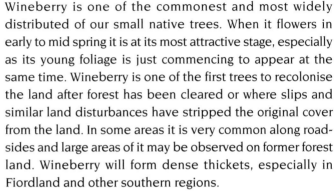

- Thin leaves sharply toothed.
- Profuse small, rosy-red flowers.

Height: 10 m

Scientific Name: *Aristotelia serrata*

Other Names: (Maori) makomako

Wineberry is one of the commonest and most widely distributed of our small native trees. When it flowers in early to mid spring it is at its most attractive stage, especially as its young foliage is just commencing to appear at the same time. Wineberry is one of the first trees to recolonise the land after forest has been cleared or where slips and similar land disturbances have stripped the original cover from the land. In some areas it is very common along roadsides and large areas of it may be observed on former forest land. Wineberry will form dense thickets, especially in Fiordland and other southern regions.

It will grow to about 10 m tall, while the trunks of mature trees can be up to 30–40 cm in diameter. The bark of more mature trees varies from quite a dark greyish-brown to almost black and the bark of young stems and that of immature trees is reddish. The opposite leaves, 5–12 cm long by 4–9 cm wide, have a thin texture; they taper to a long point and their margins are sharply toothed or serrated. The undersurfaces are often reddish or purplish, especially when young or on young trees.

The flowers, in October–November, are unisexual, the male and female flowers being produced on separate trees. They are of various tints of rosy-red while those of some trees may be greenish as they first open, changing to a rosy colour as they age. They are produced in much-branched panicles that spring from the leaf axils. Individual flowers each have four petals that are deeply cut or lobed around their margins. The shiny fruits vary from a dark red to almost black and are about 8 mm in diameter. They usually ripen between November and January, and are eaten by silvereyes, tui and New Zealand pigeons (which also consume the leaves).

Wineberry occurs in lowland to montane forests throughout the North, South (absent from the Canterbury Plains) and Stewart Islands, from sea level to about 1060 m. The wood was sometimes used for fence rails and was occasionally employed by cabinetmakers for inlay work. As the name implies, the berries were once used in making a wine, as well as jams and jellies. It was thus also formerly inappropriately known as New Zealand currant, and is sometimes known as makomako.

Hinau

■ Long leaves.

■ White, bell-shaped flowers.

Height: 10–20 m

Scientific Name:
Elaeocarpus dentatus

Hinau is a relatively tall forest tree that will grow to 10 m or possibly 20 m tall. It is tall enough to be part of the forest canopy and in more open situations has a large, rounded and much-branched head.

Its trunk may be up to 90 cm in diameter and the greyish bark is rough and fissured. The leaves are 5–12 cm long by 2–3 cm wide. Those of juvenile plants are usually longer and narrower. The leaf margins are slightly rolled downwards and are bluntly toothed with distantly spaced, small teeth. Hinau has very attractive white flowers that are about 12 mm in diameter, produced in racemes up to 10 cm or more long. The tips of the petals are toothed or incised, a feature that gives the flowers a very dainty appearance. Flowering is in October–December. The purple or purplish-grey fruits are up to 1.8 cm long and generally ripen December–May, when they are taken by New Zealand pigeons.

Hinau is found in lowland forests throughout the North and South Islands from near North Cape to the Catlins River in Otago but is absent from the Canterbury Plains. It occurs from sea level to 600 m. Hinau wood is a light, dull grey with the heartwood being darker. It was, apparently, never in great demand but was used at times for bridge construction, railway sleepers, posts and piles.

Early Maori greatly valued hinau fruits as a source of food. A chief who owned a grove of hinau trees was considered to be a wealthy man. The fruits were unpalatable in their raw state and much work was required to prepare them for eating. They were soaked in water, in a canoe, for some time and then rubbed with the hands to break them up and assist with removing the kernels, the skins and bits of stalks, which then left a dark and oily, coarse, greyish meal. This was mixed with water and made into cakes which weighed about 10–15 kg each. Because of their size they were cooked in an umu for about two days before being ready to eat. These cakes were too oily for Pakeha tastes. The bark of the hinau is rich in tannin and was used by Maori for the extraction of a dark-blue or blue-black dye.

Pokaka

Pokaka is a canopy tree that may grow to a height of 16 m or more. One noticeable feature is that, relative to its height, the girth of its trunk can be quite large, and specimens up to a metre or so in diameter are not uncommon.

One of the most interesting features of the pokaka is that young trees go through a juvenile phase that is so distinct from the adult tree that the two might be regarded as separate species. This juvenile stage may persist for many years before the tree begins to mature. Young juveniles have a tangled mass of interlaced branchlets that appear as though the plant will never grow into a large tree. The branchlets have rather scattered leaves that are variously toothed and lobed and bear absolutely no resemblance to those of the adult. The variability of the shape these juvenile leaves can be is quite remarkable. In general, they may be around 1–5 cm long, usually quite narrow and a brownish-green to purplish-brown colour.

After some years the tree commences to change and some adult leaves appear on the uppermost branchlets. From that point onwards the tree gradually loses its interlacing, juvenile branches, although some can still persist for a number of years. The trunk of a mature tree has greyish-white bark that is finely fissured or slightly roughened and is easily recognised. The adult leaves are 3–11 cm long by 1–3 cm wide, their margins irregularly and bluntly toothed, and their upper surfaces dark green. Pokaka has greenish-white flowers, borne in long, slender racemes. They are similar to those of the hinau but not nearly as attractive.

Pokaka wood was never highly valued and had only limited uses. The fruits of the pokaka are smaller, about 1.8 cm long, and are similar to those of hinau. Although edible, they would have required a far greater effort in order to provide much as much food as could be obtained from a hinau. Pokaka occurs in lowland to montane forests, in the North Island from about Mangonui southwards and then throughout the South and Stewart Islands. It ranges from sea level to 1050 m.

Mountain ribbonwood (*Hoheria glabrata*)

- Deciduous; leaves yellow in autumn.
- Profuse white flowers in January.

Height: 10 m

Scientific Name: *Hoheria glabrata*

Other Names: Ribbonwood, lacebark; (Maori) houhi

Mountain ribbonwood is confined to the South Island and as well as having the distinction of being one of our few deciduous trees, it is also one of the very few native trees that has autumn colour. Mountain ribbonwood is a small tree to perhaps 10 m tall, and it is often, but not always, branched from its base and may have several main trunks. While its bark is relatively smooth, it is usually covered by mosses and lichens.

The leaves are 5–14 cm long by about 10 cm wide and they are toothed around their margins. Their apexes are narrowed to long points that are generally referred to as 'drip tips' as they facilitate the run-off of rainwater to the forest floor. Especially at higher altitudes its leaves turn a lovely yellow during the autumn. Its beautiful white flowers are about 4 cm in diameter and are produced from the leaf axils and may be solitary or in clusters of 2–5. In full flower, the mountain ribbonwood is an outstanding tree that cannot fail to catch the eye. Flowering usually occurs in January when it enlivens some areas with the profusion of its wonderful blossoms.

Mountain ribbonwood occurs in lowland and subalpine forests throughout the higher rainfall regions about and west of the main divide of the South Island. It ascends from near sea level to 1060 m. It is distinguished from its close relative H. *lyallii* because its branchlets, leaves and leaf stalks are smooth and hairless.

Although also known as lacebark, mountain ribbonwood is the name most generally used for this species, but trampers, mountaineers and the like commonly abbreviate it to just ribbonwood. The Maori name for this species is houhi but it is seldom used.

Mountain ribbonwood (*Hoheria lyallii*)

- Branchlets, leaves and stalks have fine hairs.
- Hairs give leaves a whitish appearance.

Height: 6 m

Scientific Name: *Hoheria lyallii*

Other Names: Ribbonwood; (Maori) whauwhi

The principal differences between *Hoheria lyallii* and *H. glabrata* are that the branchlets, leaves and leaf stalks of *H. lyallii* are densely covered with fine hairs and this species is confined to the drier eastern ranges, east of the main divide, that are less influenced by the westerly rainfall. *Hoheria lyallii* is also usually a somewhat smaller tree than *H. glabrata*.

If the hairs on the leaves and stems are closely examined with a hand lens it will be noticed that they are distinctly star-shaped, and so dense is the covering of those hairs that the leaves often have a whitish, hoary appearance. The leaves are 5–10 cm long by 2–5 cm wide and their margins have similar toothing to those of *H. glabrata*. Its white flowers are up to 4 cm in diameter and, as with *H. glabrata*, are produced from the leaf axils in 2–5-flowered clusters. The tree reaches to about 6 m high.

Hoheria lyallii occurs in montane and subalpine forest of the South Island, along streams and streamsides and around forest margins, from near Blenheim to northern Central Otago. It ranges from 360 m to 900 m in altitude. In some areas it is not uncommonly seen in open country, such as along high-country streams or on shingle fans, and can be most noticeable because of the hoary appearance of its leaves and its conspicuous white flowers.

Trampers, mountaineers and high-country folk do not differentiate between this species and *H. glabrata*, both being simply referred to as ribbonwood. The Maori name for this species is whauwhi but it is seldom used. Botanical opinion is split as to whether the two species should be regarded as two distinct entities or united under the one species as *H. glabrata*.

Lacebark

Leaves shiny, prominent veins, sharply toothed.

Flower scent fills air in late summer.

Height: 6–15 m

Scientific Name: *Hoheria populnea*

Other Names: Ribbonwood; (Maori) houhere, houi, whauwhi

Lacebark is a rather variable species that is confined to the upper part of the North Island from about North Cape southwards to the Waikato region and the Bay of Plenty.

It will grow to about 6–15 m tall, while its trunk seldom attains 60 cm in diameter. Particularly in its young state, it makes very rapid growth, sapling trees having very narrow, whippy stems. It has greyish-brown bark that is slightly roughened and its stems are generally quite difficult to break because of its layered bark making it quite tough and stringy. Young plants may have quite a variable appearance, and their leaves may differ so much from those of the adult that it is often difficult to recognise them as belonging to the same species.

The adult lacebark leaves are 7.5–14 cm long by 3–6 cm wide, their upper surfaces shiny and some of the veins are often also quite prominent. Their margins are rather coarsely toothed. The leaves provide food for New Zealand pigeons as part of their winter diet. When the lacebark flowers it then becomes most noticeable. The white flowers are up to 2.5 cm in diameter, strongly scented, and are produced either singly or in 5–10-flowered axillary clusters. Flowering usually occurs during the late summer or autumn and the surrounding air is often pervaded by the strength of their perfume. As the flowers fade they are then replaced by its distinctive seed cases. There are five seeds per flower and each seed case has five prominent wings so as to aid dispersal once the seeds ripen in mid-autumn to early winter.

The lacebark goes by a variety of names including houi, whauwhi, ribbonwood and houhere. The last name has given rise to its scientific name (*Hoheria*), which is now used almost exclusively instead of its other common names. It used also to be referred to as thousand-jacket, in reference to the various layers of its inner bark. This inner fibre is remarkably tough and was formerly used as cordage, for tying bundles and the like. It also is attractively perforated and has been used for ornamental purposes such as trimming ladies' hats and for basketwork.

Long-leaved lacebark

■ **Longest and narrowest leaves of** *Hoheria* **species.**

■ **Sweetly scented, showy white flowers from late summer.**

Height: 8 m

Scientific Name:
Hoheria sexstylosa

Other Names:
(Maori) hoheria,
houhere

This is the commonest species of lacebark and occurs over quite a wide area of the North Island from about the Kaipara Harbour southwards. In the South Island it occurs from north-western Nelson to a little north of Greymouth, on Banks Peninsula and it has also been recorded near Gore. Often it is commonly found around the margins of forest.

Known as the long-leaved lacebark because its leaves are generally longer and narrower than those of lacebark (H. *populnea*), it occurs in lowland to lower montane forests from sea level to 760 m.

Generally, it is slightly smaller in growth than the other *Hoheria* species, seldom attaining a height more that 8 m and its trunk is rarely more than 40 cm in diameter. The adult leaves of this species will grow to about 18 cm in length (occasionally longer on some forms) and they can also be quite variable. Its longer, narrower leaves help to distinguish it from H. *populnea*. Also its flowers are produced singly or, generally, in clusters of 2–5 flowers. The seed cases are formed following flowering and they usually have six (occasionally seven) wings formed from each flower. The species' scientific name of *sexstylosa* refers to the fact that the flowers generally have six styles and are therefore capable of developing six seeds.

As with lacebark, it is extremely showy when in flower and its flowers are also very sweetly scented. Flowering generally commences during late summer and may continue until early autumn.

The long-leaved lacebark has sometimes been recorded from other South Island localities but, in such instances, it generally turns out that it was probably planted in those localities many years ago, so that it now gives the impression that it is actually native to those areas.

Lowland ribbonwood

- **Our largest deciduous tree.**

- **Twiggy juvenile stage.**

Height: 6–20 m

Scientific Name: *Plagianthus regius*

Other Names: Ribbonwood; (Maori) houi (Stewart Is., Chatham Is.), manatu

As well as being one of the few deciduous trees native to New Zealand, lowland ribbonwood is also the largest of our deciduous trees. It forms a spreading crown and will attain heights of 6–20 m with a trunk up to 1 m in diameter. On young trees the bark is usually smooth and dark brown, but on older trees it can have quite a rough and warted texture.

As a young plant it has a rather twiggy juvenile stage with interlacing branchlets and has a very different appearance from that of the adult. The leaves of juvenile trees are ovate or rounded and usually widely spaced on the branchlets. On older trees the leaves are 2.5–7.5 cm long by 2–5 cm wide and they have a rather soft texture. Their margins are also conspicuously and irregularly toothed and lobed. When the new foliage is produced in spring and is closely followed by the male flowers the trees are at their most attractive.

The male and female flowers are produced on separate trees, although sometimes trees with flowers of both sexes may be found. The flowers are produced in repeatedly branched, terminal panicles up to 23 cm long. While the individual flowers are quite small, collectively they can make quite an impact, the male flowers being the showiest. They are a most attractive lime-green colour, each little flower being surrounded by five small petals and having a cluster of small, pale creamy anthers at their centres. The female flowers are smaller and do not have the conspicuous petals of the male. The seed capsules are produced on the female trees, each capsule containing just one seed.

Although widely distributed throughout most of the country, there are some districts from which the tree may be almost or quite absent. It occurs in lowland forests from Mangonui and Kaitaia southwards to Stewart Island as well as on the Chatham Islands. It extends from sea level to about 450 m.

The wood was little used because it was not durable. Various common names have been applied to the species, from houi on Stewart and Chatham Islands to manatu, especially in the North Island, and ribbonwood throughout the South Island; however, to distinguish it from the *Hoheria* species, also known as ribbonwood, it is usually known as lowland ribbonwood. Early Maori used the inner fibres of the bark for making rope and twine for their fishing nets.

Kamahi

- **Thick, leathery, shiny leaves.**
- **Profuse clusters of flowers from spring.**

Height: 25–30 m

Scientific Name: *Weinmannia racemosa*

Other Names: (Maori) tawhero (East Cape)

Kamahi is commonly found throughout much of New Zealand, occurring in lowland to montane forests of the North Island from the mid-Waikato and lower Coromandel southwards and then throughout the South Island (except for the Canterbury Plains, North and Central Otago) and on Stewart Island. After the forest has been felled, kamahi is often one of the main trees to regenerate, particularly in Westland. It occurs from sea level to about 900 m.

It is a medium to tall forest tree and will grow quite tall, 25–30 m being not uncommon. The largest specimens may have trunks 30 cm–1.2 m in diameter. Its bark is relatively smooth and light-coloured, usually being whitish or grey. The quite thick and leathery leaves are 3–10 cm long by 2–4 cm wide, deep green and shiny, and their margins are coarsely and bluntly toothed. On seedling trees the leaves are thin and pliable and are either simple (not divided into leaflets) or have up to three leaflets and, frequently, they are a strong red in colour. At that stage the cut branchlets are valued by florists. Kamahi flowers very profusely, between October and January, and is valued by apiarists because of the finely flavoured honey that is produced from its abundant nectar. Its white flowers are borne on racemes that are up to 11 cm long. The individual flowers are very feathery and consist mainly of long stamens, the petals being quite small and inconspicuous.

Kamahi wood is deep red and was used by cabinetmakers because of its very ornamental nature. It was also used for a variety of other purposes such a house blocks, piles, tramway sleepers and general construction. The bark was also considerably valued for tanning purposes. *Weinmannia racemosa* was known in the East Cape area as tawhero, a name that is more generally applied to the related *W. silvicola*. Throughout most of the country it is now known as kamahi, but some of the bushmen of the 19th century commonly, and indiscriminately, used to refer to it as red birch or brown birch. In parts of the North Island the common name has been corrupted into kamai instead of kamahi.

Towai

Towai is a handsome tree that will grow 6–25 m tall. Its trunk may vary from 60 to 90 cm in diameter and, while it has similarities with the kamahi, this species is easily distinguished on account of its leaves which, on mature trees, comprise up to five pairs of leaflets plus one relatively large terminal leaflet.

The leaves of adult trees are 4–7 cm long by 2–3 cm wide. The leaflets are quite thick and leathery, upper surfaces being deep green and shiny, and they have coarsely and bluntly toothed margins. As a juvenile tree it can be quite confusing because its leaves vary so much, from being partly simple (not divided into leaflets) to those that have several pairs of leaflets or even just three leaflets. Towai flowers are rather similar to those of the kamahi, the flower racemes being up to 10 cm long. Like the kamahi it flowers between late summer and mid-autumn.

Towai is confined to northern New Zealand, being found in lowland forests and around forest margins from Mangonui to Waikato and the Bay of Plenty. It ascends from sea level to 900 m. Towai wood is a light, brownish-red with an even and compact grain, which has been used for ornamental work, while the bark was highly favoured during the 19th century for use in tanneries as it contained 10–13 per cent tannin. This is not as much as some other trees have but it is still a reasonable percentage. Towai is also known as tawhero.

Putaputaweta

■ Light- and dark-green marbling on leaves.

■ Panicles of small, white flowers.

Height: 10 m

Scientific Name: *Carpodetus serratus*

Other Names: Marbleleaf

Putaputaweta is quite common and it is found throughout the three main islands, with the exception of the Canterbury Plains and North and Central Otago. It is a small to medium tree of spreading habit and rarely grows taller than 10 m with a trunk up to 30 cm in diameter. The bark is pale greyish and somewhat roughened. Weta are commonly found living in holes in the trunk of North Island trees, the holes originally bored by puriri moth caterpillars.

The leaves are 2.5–6 cm long by 1.5–3 cm wide. Their upper surfaces are characterised by a distinctive light- and dark-green marbling which gives rise to one of its common names of marbleleaf. The leaf margins have small, sharp teeth. Putaputaweta has small, white flowers that are about 6 mm in diameter, produced in many-flowered, broad, flat panicles up to 5 cm across. Generally, the flowers occur between November and January. Its small, rounded fruits are about 6 mm in diameter and they are purplish-black when ripe. They normally take almost 12 months to ripen so that ripe fruits from the previous year may be seen on the tree at the same time as the new season's flowers. Juvenile trees of the putaputaweta have a very open habit with zigzagging branchlets and smaller leaves.

Putaputaweta is found in coastal and montane forests from near North Cape to Stewart Island, especially on the banks of creeks and around the margins of forests. It ascends from sea level to 1000 m. Because its freshly cut wood was so sappy that it would not easily burn, it was sometimes given the name of bucket-of-water tree. It has also had a variety of other common names, some of which result from its resemblance to other native trees, and others which are just plain misleading: mapau, white mapau, white maple and white birch being some of them. *Carpodetus serratus* has the distinction of being the only species of its genus in New Zealand.

Westland quintinia

▮ Leaves undulating, tinged purplish-bronze.

▮ Long flower racemes in spring.

Height: 12 m

Scientific Name: *Quintinia acutifolia*

The common name of this species suggests that it is mainly found in the South Island, but nothing is further from the truth. It does, in fact, occur over quite a large part of the country. In the North Island it can be found from the Great and Little Barrier Islands to the Coromandel Peninsula and then southwards to East Cape and central Taranaki, while in the South Island it occurs in north-western Nelson and then southwards through Westland to about the Fox Glacier. The Westland quintinia is fairly common in forests along the west of the South Island and usually ranges from sea level to 760 m.

It is a rather bushy tree up to 12 m tall and with a trunk that may be up to 60 cm in diameter. The leaves are from 6–16 cm long by 2–5 cm wide. While their margins are not as strongly undulating as those of the tawheowheo they have similar, small but distant teeth. Their upper surfaces are green and shiny and may often be tinged purplish-bronze. The undersurfaces are quite pale.

Although quite unrelated to *Weinmannia* both species of *Quintinia* dealt with here have flower racemes that look remarkably similar to those of kamahi. Its small, white flowers are produced on racemes up to 10 cm long, usually between October and November.

Tawheowheo

All three of New Zealand's species of *Quintinia* (only two are dealt with here) are rather similar but the main difference between the Westland quintinia and the tawheowheo is the size and shape of the leaves. Tawheowheo leaves are narrower, being of the narrow-lanceolate to narrow-oblong order, whereas those of the Westland quintinia are distinctly wider, being obovate to broad-elliptic and usually 3–5 cm wide.

Tawheowheo forms a small, openly branched tree, usually no more than 14 m tall, and its trunk may be up to 50 cm or so in diameter. The leaves are 6–12.5 cm long by 1–2.5 cm wide. They are usually a greenish-yellow and marked with green and reddish blotches. Their undulating margins are distantly and coarsely toothed. One of its distinctive features is that the old leaves often turn a bright red before they fall. The racemes of small, white flowers are similar to those of the Westland quintinia, and are 6–8 cm long.

The tree occurs only in the North Island from Mangonui southwards to northern Taranaki and Poverty Bay, growing in lowland and montane forests from sea level to 1050 m.

The wood of the tawheowheo is light red in colour and is often attractively figured. It has been used by cabinetmakers but was never available in sufficient quantity for more general use. In the East Cape district the tree used to be called kumarahou, a name which now appears to have fallen into disuse. The name of tawheowheo is sometimes corrupted to tawherowhero, which has no significance whatsoever.

Kowhai *(Sophora microphylla)*

- **Bright yellow flowers.**

- **Brown seed pods.**

Height: 10 m

Scientific Name: *Sophora microphylla*

Kowhai is one of our most spectacular native trees and it can justifiably claim to be our national flower. *Sophora* is quite a variable genus with at least seven different species of kowhai that are now recognised; however, to the layperson, most of them are of a fairly similar appearance and they are all simply referred to as kowhai.

The common species (*S. microphylla*) is one of the most widely distributed and the one most likely to be seen. It occurs over much of the North Island and over virtually all of the South Island, along river banks, around lake shores, on forest outskirts and in open places in lowland and lower montane regions. It ascends from sea level to 760 m.

Kowhai is a very variable species and it is quite common for each district to have its own variations as far as habit is concerned. In some areas (particularly the eastern South Island) it is common for young kowhai trees to go through a rather tangled and twiggy, divaricating form in a juvenile stage that may last for up to 15 years or more. In other districts, that juvenile phase is less marked. Kowhai will grow to about 10 m or more with a trunk up to 60 cm in diameter. The bark is rough and furrowed and generally a greyish or grey-brown in colour.

On adult trees the leaves are 7.5–15 cm long and generally have 20–40 pairs of leaflets; each is usually less than 1 cm long. Flowering can be equally variable, in some districts commencing as early as July, while in others it can be any time from September to late October or even early November. The flowers are up to 4.5 cm long and are produced on 4–10-flowered racemes. The seed pods are 7.5–15 cm long with four narrow wings. At first the pods are green but they soon change to brown. Kowhai seeds are first a yellowish-green but as the pods age they change to a deep yellow and very old seeds become almost brown in colour.

Although its common name kowhai, also applied to the colour yellow in Maori, is used throughout New Zealand, it has been subject to numerous local variations. The pale brown kowhai wood is very dense and compact, and was once much used for fence posts and similar purposes. It is greatly valued by wood turners.

Kowhai (*Sophora tetraptera*)

- Restricted to East Coast region.

- Flowers and leaflets larger than *S. microphylla*.

Height: 12 m

Scientific Name: *Sophora tetraptera*

Sophora tetraptera has a rather restricted distribution, being found only in the North Island from the East Cape area southwards to the Ruahine Range. It is found in similar habitats to S. *microphylla*, such as along streamsides, around forest margins as well as in open places of lowland and hill-country areas, ranging from sea level to 450 m.

This species is distinguished from S. *microphylla* by not passing through any distinct juvenile or divaricating stage. Initially, it has rather stiff and erect growth but will eventually develop a more spreading habit of growth. This kowhai will grow to about 12 m tall and, on larger specimens, the trunk can be up to 60 cm in diameter. Its greyish-brown bark is rough and furrowed.

The leaves are 7.5–16 cm long and they generally have 10–20 pairs of leaflets. These much larger leaflets, 1.5–3.5 cm long, also distinguish this kowhai. Its flowers are also larger, being up to 5.7 cm long and they are produced on 4–10-flowered racemes. Their flowers are full of nectar and, when in season, are a great favourite with tui, bellbirds and silvereyes. The flowers of the kowhai at first open a greenish-yellow but as they mature they change to a rich gold. The seed pods are up to 20 cm long and their wings are broader than those of S. *microphylla* (see the notes under S. *microphylla*, p. 106, for seed development).

While the kowhai is evergreen, trees often tend to drop much of their foliage just before flowering commences. Once flowering has been completed, the tree bursts forth into its new foliage. S. *tetraptera* and S. *microphylla* may also be distinguished by their flowers. Kowhai flowers comprise four parts: the lower petal or keel, two side petals or wings and the upper petal or standard. In S. *tetraptera* the standard is distinctly shorter than its wings. On the other hand, the length of the standard of S. *microphylla* is about equal to its two wings.

Kowhai has some medicinal properties and was used by Maori for applying as a poultice to wounds and tumours; an infusion made from the bark of kowhai together with manuka bark was apparently used to treat internal pains, bruises and broken limbs. The ashes from the wood were used for the treatment of ringworm.

Red beech

Buttresses at base.

Sharp teeth on leaf margins.

Height: 30 m

Scientific Name: *Nothofagus fusca*

Other Names: (Maori) tawhairaunui

The red beech is one of our nobler trees as well as being one of the tallest. It will attain heights of 30 m or more, its tall, straight trunks being up to 2 m or so in diameter. To venture through some prime red beech forest such as on the Lewis Pass highway or in the Eglinton Valley of Fiordland is an experience to be treasured.

Red beech has shaggy, dark-brown bark and one of its characteristic features is that the base of the trunk often has prominent, plank-like buttresses. Its leaves are 2–4 cm long by 2–2.5 cm wide and are distinguished by having 6–8 pairs of coarse, sharp teeth around the upper two-thirds of their margins. This toothing also helps to distinguish red beech from hard beech (*Nothofagus truncata*), which has 8–12 pairs of blunt teeth around the upper three-quarters of their margins. The leaves of old red beech often turn red before they fall, while the foliage of seedling trees frequently turns a deep red, especially during the winter months.

The beech trees have separate male and female flowers but they do not always flower well every year. When they do flower (and fruit) well it is known as a 'mast year' and at these times the seeds provide such a plentiful amount of food that mice, rats and other pests may assume plague proportions in beech forests.

The male flowers are rather small, being in clusters of 1–8 per branchlet, and, on the red beech, their yellow- or straw-coloured anthers (occasionally reddish) make them quite conspicuous. The female flowers are usually in groups of 1–5 per branchlet but they are not usually as conspicuous. The fruits are small cupules, about 1 cm long, in which sit the nut-like seeds.

Red beech occurs in lowland and montane forests from near Te Aroha and Rotorua southwards to Southland and Fiordland, except for the Canterbury Plains. It ascends from sea level to 1060 m. Along with the other species of *Nothofagus*, red beech is absent from Mt Taranaki. Collectively, the *Nothofagus* (meaning false beech) species are known as southern beeches (to distinguish them from the northern-hemisphere beeches). Red beech is also known as tawhairaunui, and in earlier times had a whole raft of other common names, including red birch. The wood is red in colour, straight-grained and quite well figured. It is now mainly used for furniture manufacture.

Silver beech

▮ Silvery white bark.

▮ Thick, leathery leaves with blunt teeth.

Height: 30 m

Scientific Name: *Nothofagus menziesii*

Other Names: (Maori) tawhai

Among the native beech trees, silver beech is very easily recognised. It is quite a large tree but perhaps not as majestic as the red beech. Silver beech has a dense and wide-spreading, bushy crown and will attain heights of up to 30 m. Its trunk can be up to 2 m or more in diameter and it sometimes shows buttressing at its base but possibly not as prominently as the red beech. The bark of young trees is silvery-white and that may have given rise to its common name of silver beech. As the trunk ages it becomes rather grey and shaggy. Quite often it is densely covered with mosses and lichens.

The leaves are 8–20 mm long by 7–12 mm wide, thick and leathery, and their margins are doubly toothed with blunt teeth. In the spring the young foliage is a most attractive pale green. The male flowers are borne 1–4 per stalk and they are greenish to straw-coloured. The female flowers are also 1–4 per stalk but are produced closer to the tips of the branchlets than the males. The nuts sit inside small cupules.

In the North Island, silver beech occurs in lowland and montane forests from near Thames and Te Aroha southwards to the Tararua Range (absent from Mt Taranaki). It occurs throughout much of the South Island except in east coast areas. Often it may be no more than a stunted shrub in subalpine areas. It ranges from sea level to about 900 m.

Silver beech wood is deep red in colour and while it is compact and dense it is not well figured. It main use is for manufacturing furniture, although it has been used as a general utility timber.

As with the other species of *Nothofagus*, silver beech has, at various times, been known by a variety of common names, many of which are of no more than historical value, but its more generally accepted alternative name is tawhai.

Black beech

■ Dominant in upper South Island forest.

■ Bark often has black fungus.

Height: 20–25 m

Scientific Name:
Nothofagus solandri

Black beech occurs in lowland and montane forests over much of central New Zealand, from the East Cape and Mamaku Plateau in the North Island, then southwards to southern Westland and South Canterbury. It ascends from sea level to 760 m and, like other N*othofagus* species, is absent from Mt Taranaki. Particularly in the northern half of the South Island, it is a characteristic tree that covers the mountainous landscape with a uniform mantle of deep green.

It can be quite a tall tree, sometimes reaching 30 m, but usually 20–25 m; it may have a trunk up to 1 m in diameter. The rough bark is grey and furrowed but is often concealed by a black fungus that gives this tree its common name. On young trees the bark is frequently rather smooth.

Black beech is host to a native scale insect that exudes honeydew which encourages the growth of a black, sooty-mould fungus. The honeydew provides kaka and bellbirds with an essential source of food, but unfortunately also provides sustenance for two introduced wasps so that they rob the native birds of their traditional food.

The leaves are 7–20 cm long by 4–10 mm wide. Their upper surfaces are deep green and somewhat shiny and the undersurfaces are pale. Generally, their tips are blunt, but because this species not infrequently hybridises with other beeches, the blunt tip is not always a reliable character for identification.

The male flowers often have bright red anthers so that when a tree has a good flowering year it can be very colourful. As is typical of the beeches, it does not flower well every year. The quite small female flowers are produced near the tips of the branchlets in 1–3-flowered clusters. The nuts are 7 mm long and sit in a small cupule.

As with the other species of beech, the old-time bushmen gave this tree a variety of common names including white birch, red birch and brown birch. These names were the cause of a great deal of confusion because nobody knew to which species of beech they were referring. Black beech wood is a pale red colour, sometimes greyish, often streaked with black and sometimes attractively figured. It is tough and strong but is not durable in exposed situations. The foothills of North Canterbury were the source of the considerable quantity of black beech timber used in the late 19th century.

Mountain beech

- **Leaves sharply pointed.**
- **Greyish-white hairs beneath leaves.**

Height: 15 m

Scientific Name:
Nothofagus solandri var. *cliffortioides*

In general appearance mountain beech is very similar to black beech, but mountain beech is generally a smaller tree and its leaves are sharply pointed. The veining on the leaves of mountain beech is usually rather obscure and its margins are generally rolled slightly downwards. Hybridism between the two species can sometimes make it difficult to tell which species is which.

Usually, mountain beech is a small tree, up to 15 m or so, but taller trees, up to 30 m, may occur in other areas, particularly in western Southland. The trunk may be up to 60 cm in diameter but specimens with trunks up to 1 m in diameter have been recorded. Generally, its bark is smooth but becomes rough and furrowed on older trees. In drier habitats the trunks of mountain beech may often be covered with sooty mould.

The leaves (see inset photo) are 1–1.5 cm long by 7–10 mm wide and their undersurfaces are clad with a greyish-white tomentum whereas those of the black beech are smooth and have no tomentum. Their upper surfaces are dark green and shiny. The male flowers are produced in groups of 3–4 per branchlet and, like the black beech, they often have red anthers. The female flowers are produced near the tips of the branchlets in groups of 1–2.

Mountain beech occurs, in the North Island, in montane and subalpine forests from near East Cape southwards, but is absent from Mt Taranaki and the Tararua Range. It occurs throughout much of the South Island and often covers many kilometres of hill and mountain with its unvarying dark green. It ascends from sea level to 1220 m. For some unknown reason the species of *Nothofagus* never managed to cross Foveaux Strait so that there are no beech trees on Stewart Island. Although not durable in exposed conditions, numbers of mountain huts have been constructed with poles of mountain beech, cut from the bush, and quite often they lasted for a good number of years.

Hard beech

Probably the least known of the beech species is *Nothofagus truncata*, the hard beech. It is actually a large forest tree and will attain heights of up to 30 m and have a trunk that may be up to 2 m or so in diameter. As with some of the other beech species, the base of its trunk can be prominently buttressed. Its bark varies from dark slate-grey to blackish and is rough and furrowed. Like black beech, honeydew on the bark produced by a scale insect provides food for birds and insects and encourages the growth of a sooty mould.

The leaves are 2.5–3.5 cm long by about 2 cm wide. Their upper surfaces are deep green and shiny. Generally, they are rather similar to those of red beech; the most obvious difference between the two species being that the hard beech has 8–12 pairs of small, blunt teeth around the upper three-quarters of the leaf margins, whereas red beech has only 6–8 pairs of sharp teeth around the upper two-thirds of the leaf margins. Many of its leaves are shed in early spring. The male flowers of hard beech are in groups of 1–3 and the colour of the anthers varies from greenish to red. The female flowers are produced in groups of three.

Hard beech occurs in lowland and lower montane forests from Mangonui, in the far north, and then throughout most of the North Island (apart from Mt Taranaki). In the South Island it extends from Marlborough and Nelson southwards to northern Westland. It ranges from sea level to 900 m.

The wood of hard beech is pinkish, when first cut, but gradually changes to a light-brown colour. It received the name of hard beech because the wood is noticeably harder than that of the other species of beech. It was formerly used for bridge building, railway sleepers, post and poles but these days is little used. It is sometimes known as clinker beech.

Ewekuri

Ewekuri is fairly common throughout much of the North Island but in the South Island is confined to a small area around Golden Bay and the Marlborough Sounds at the very top of the island. It occurs in lowland forests from sea level to about 450 m.

It has a short trunk and forms a spreading tree, up to about 12 m in height, with a trunk up to around 60 cm in diameter. One of the interesting things about the ewekuri is that, if the bark is damaged, a milky sap is exuded. This sap is quite palatable and has been used as a substitute for milk.

The leaves of juvenile ewekuri are quite distinct from those of the adult, their margins being deeply lobed close to their bases so that they are fiddle-shaped (see lower photo). The juvenile leaves are 2–6 cm long by 1–3 cm wide. The adult leaves are 4–8 cm long by 2–3.5 cm wide and they have bluntly toothed margins that are not lobed.

Male and female flowers are borne on separate trees and are in spikes that usually arise from the leaf axils. They may be solitary, paired or sometimes in threes and the spikes are 2.5–3 cm long. The female flowers are followed by bright red, succulent fruits.

Ewekuri is sometimes known as large-leaved milk tree.

Turepo

- Smaller leaves than ewekuri.
- Juvenile form has zigzagging branches.

Height: 12 m

Scientific Name:
Streblus heterophyllus

Other Names:
Milk tree

Turepo is a relative of ewekuri (*Streblus banksii*) but differs in having much smaller leaves. It is a small tree up to 12 m or so in height with a trunk up to about 60 cm in diameter. Its bark is grey to almost white and has a rough texture.

It has a long-persisting juvenile form, of divaricating or zigzagging habit, that is quite different from the adult tree. The leaves of this juvenile form are variously lobed and quite frequently are fiddle-shaped (see lower photo). Their terminal lobes are sometimes very large. On adult trees the leaves are 8 mm–2.5 cm long by 4–12 mm wide and their margins are bluntly toothed.

As with ewekuri, the male and female flowers occur on separate trees. The flowers are produced in axillary spikes that are either solitary or paired and 1.5–2.5 cm long. The succulent fruits are bright red and about 5 mm in diameter.

Turepo is sometimes quite abundant in moist, lowland forests throughout both the North and South Islands. It favours moist areas such as along creeks and riverbanks as well as around forest margins. The species occurs from sea level to about 450 m.

Turepo is also known as the milk tree because its milky sap was sometimes used as a substitute for milk by the early settlers.

Karaka

- Very glossy, dark-green leaves.
- Large, orange fruits.

Height: 15 m

Scientific Name: *Corynocarpus laevigatus*

Other Names: (Maori) kopi (Chatham Is.)

Karaka is a bold and handsome tree that is striking at all times and is usually quite easily recognised, especially when seen growing in more open situations. It forms a medium tree, usually up to 15 m tall but occasional taller specimens may be encountered. Its trunk can be up to 60 cm or more in diameter and the grey bark is rather smooth.

The thick, leathery leaves are 10–15 cm long by 5–7 cm wide. Their upper surfaces are shiny and the midribs are slightly paler. Small, green flowers are produced in panicles up to 20 cm long, and they are followed by large fruits, around 2.5–4 cm long. When ripe they are fleshy and bright orange. Flowering occurs during spring, usually August–November and the fruits ripen January–April, depending upon locality.

Karaka is abundant in coastal and lowland forests but recent research has shown it was naturally distributed only in the northern parts of the North Island. Its wider distribution throughout the rest of the North Island and the north of the South Island was thanks to early Maori who, because they commonly cultivated it, ensured that it was spread around the country. It now occurs throughout the North Island and in the South Island as far south as Greymouth and Banks Peninsula. Often it is associated with old habitation sites. It also occurs on the Chatham Islands.

Karaka was highly important to Maori as a source of food. Groves of karaka trees were highly valued and were strictly tapu. The flesh of the fruits could be eaten raw, but the kernels were bitter, unpalatable and very toxic, so that they required some preparation before they could be eaten. They were soaked in water before being placed in a large umu (earth oven) and then steam-baked for several hours so as to remove their toxicity. Next they were washed in running water to remove the husks and the fibrous matter that coats the kernels, and to ensure all traces of toxicity had disappeared. Once washed, they were then dried and stored. When required for use, the kernels were again steamed. On the Chatham Islands the kernels were known as kopi, as was the whole tree. Karaka fruit is eaten by New Zealand pigeons.

Kaikomako

- Juvenile has interlacing branches.

- Profuse, fragrant white flowers.

Height: 12 m

Scientific Name:
Pennantia corymbosa

Kaikomako is a canopy tree that will attain heights of around 12 m, although usually it is quite a bit smaller. Its trunk is usually rather slender and the bark of older trees is greyish and slightly roughened.

The tree undergoes a distinct juvenile phase quite different from that of the adult. It commences life as a divaricating shrub, with interlacing branchlets and small, wedge-shaped leaves that more often than not are a brownish colour. This juvenile phase may last 10 years before the tree begins to show signs of assuming its adult form.

On the adult tree, the leaves are 5–10 cm long by 1–4 cm wide, oblong to obovate-oblong; their upper surfaces are medium to deep green and shiny, and their margins coarsely toothed.

Kaikomako frequently has separate male and female flowers on different trees, although sometimes it will also produce perfect flowers (male and female together) on the one tree. When a kaikomako tree flowers well, it literally smothers itself with flowers. Its white flowers, produced November–February, have a rather waxy appearance and a lovely fragrance. The fruits are about 8–9 mm long and they are usually a blackish colour when ripe. They are popular with whiteheads and bellbirds (kaikomako translates as 'food of the bellbird').

Kaikomako occurs in lowland and hilly forests throughout the North and South Islands. In the North Island it occurs from Kaitaia southwards and in the South Island it is absent from the Canterbury Plains as well as North and Central Otago. It ranges from sea level to about 600 m.

Because of its hard wood, kaikomako was one of the trees that was used by Maori for generating fire by friction. A piece of dry kaikomako wood was sharpened to a point and then rubbed very vigorously backwards and forwards along a block of a softer wood, such as mahoe or pate. Gradually, a groove was formed and, after much effort, a small ball of fluff would form at one end of the groove from which, if it became hot enough, a flame could be kindled.

Kaikomako wood is light-coloured, straight in the grain and very hard. It was never available in any quantity for commercial use but was sometimes used for ornamental work by cabinetmakers.

Kohekohe

Kohekohe is one of the most striking of our native trees but, unfortunately, as a result of forest clearance and the ravages of the introduced brush-tailed possum, it is now much less common than it used to be. It once formed extensive areas of coastal and lowland forest throughout much of the North Island and in the northern part of the South Island.

It is a distinctive tree that has a tropical appearance and is not likely to be mistaken for any other species. Kohekohe will form a round-headed tree to about 16 m tall and its trunk may be 90 cm–1.2 m in diameter. It has rather pale and smooth bark. The rather large leaves are on 4 cm stalks; the blades are 13–45 cm long by 3–7.5 cm wide and pinnate with 3–4 pairs of leaflets. They are medium to deep green and have shiny upper surfaces. On some of the offshore islands its leaves may be exceptionally large.

Kohekohe exhibits a character, not uncommon in tropical trees, in that it has cauliflorous inflorescences: the flowering stems are produced directly from the bare trunk and branches and not from among the foliage. The white flowers are produced on drooping inflorescences that are up to 30 cm long. Flowering usually occurs during autumn and early winter. Bellbirds feed on the nectar. The rounded fruits (see lower photo) are up to 2.5 cm in diameter and when ripe (ripening may take up to 15 months), they split open to reveal the scarlet flesh that encloses the seeds.

Kohekohe occurs in lowland forests throughout the North Island from North Cape southwards. In the South Island it is more restricted, occurring only in the Marlborough Sounds and some adjacent localities in eastern Nelson. It ranges from sea level to 450 m.

The wood of kohekohe is a pale red when seasoned, and is said to resemble Honduras mahogany. Maori fashioned it into canoes and later it was used by cabinetmakers but was never available in sufficient quantity for it to be much employed for other purposes. It was formerly, and confusingly, known as cedar. An infusion of the leaves was sometimes used by bushmen as a remedy for stomach complaints.

Titoki

- **4–6 pairs of leaflets.**
- **Furry-brown seed capsules; shiny black seeds.**

Height:
12–20 m

Scientific Name:
Alectryon excelsus

Titoki is not uncommon in the North Island and the northern half of the South Island. It is a handsome tree growing 12–20 m tall and its trunk may be up to 1 m in diameter. It occurs in coastal and lowland forests around the North Island and in the South Island to as far south as Banks Peninsula in the east and possibly to about Bruce Bay in the west. It tends to favour alluvial ground such river flats and, not infrequently, it will form isolated groves comprised almost entirely of titoki. It ascends from sea level to about 600 m.

Titoki leaves are from 10–30 cm long and have 4–6 pairs of leaflets. Each leaflet is 5–10 cm long by 2–5 cm wide and their margins vary from being toothed to more or less without any teeth. The brownish flowers of titoki are very small and are borne on much-branched panicles produced from the leaf axils. Perfect (male and female together) and unisexual (separate male and female) flowers may be produced on the same tree. Flowering usually occurs between November and December.

Its seeds can take up to a year to ripen; each seed being enclosed in a two-valved, furry-brown capsule. When ripe, the capsule splits open to reveal a jet-black seed that is partially enclosed in a fleshy, scarlet aril or receptacle that has a granulated surface (see inset photo). New Zealand pigeons and other native birds eat the fruit.

Oil squeezed from the seeds was highly valued by Maori as a hair oil and for medicinal purposes, applied externally. The wood of the titoki is of great strength and toughness, and very straight-grained. It is a light, reddish colour but is not well figured. It was used where great strength was required, particularly for tool handles and similar purposes, and was particularly used by wheelwrights and coach builders.

In the southern parts of the country, titoki was known as titongi; titoki being the northern version of its name. In some districts it was known as tokitoki, and among the settlers it was sometimes referred to as New Zealand ash on account of its foliage and the toughness of it wood resembling that of the European ash (*Fraxinus*).

Akeake

- Long, narrow leaves, rough to touch.
- Reddish-brown, peeling bark.

Height: 2–7 m

Scientific Name: *Dodonaea viscosa*

The Maori name of this tree means 'for ever and ever', referring to the fact that it has very hard, dense, long-lasting wood. It was once used for the manufacture of various kinds of clubs, especially those used for warfare.

It is a small tree of erect habit, usually 2–7 m tall, although occasionally it may grow taller. Its trunk seldom exceeds 30 cm in diameter. It is characterised by its trunk and main branches having a distinctive reddish-brown bark that is somewhat thin and peels off in rather long strips.

The young branchlets and leaves at times can be quite viscid or sticky, hence its specific name of *viscosa*. The pale green leaves of the akeake are 4–10 cm long by 1–3 cm wide and their upper surfaces are somewhat shiny. Its flowers are quite small, having no petals, and they are produced from the tips of the branchlets in densely flowered panicles. While the male and female flowers are frequently produced on separate plants, there are some trees that have both sexes on the one plant and are self-fertile. Flowering usually occurs during October and November.

Akeake fruits are conspicuous and very attractive, being a hop-like capsule with 2–3 broad wings. Before they ripen, they are an attractive lime-green, changing to a light brown as they ripen. In early to mid-summer they can be a conspicuous feature of the plant.

The akeake is common in coastal to lowland scrub and forests throughout the North Island and in the South Island as far south as Banks Peninsula in the east and to a little south of Greymouth in the west.

Akeake heartwood is generally black, marked with streaks and patches of white. Being a small tree it was never available in any quantity but was formerly valued by cabinetmakers, especially for picture frames and inlay work. At least three other species of native tree are also known by the name of akeake.

Five-finger

Five-finger is one of the commonest native trees and occurs, in the North Island, from North Cape to Wellington, and in the South Island in coastal forest to Banks Peninsula, in the east, and to about Greymouth in the west. It then reappears in North Otago, a little to the north of Dunedin, and it finally disappears at Tautuku in the Catlins District. South of Otago its place is taken by one of the varieties of *Pseudopanax colensoi* which is a much hardier species.

Five-finger is a small tree that often has several main stems, usually of somewhat gnarled appearance. It will grow to about 8 m tall and, in more open situations, forms quite a wide-spreading tree. On younger trees its bark is usually smooth, but that of older trees is rather corky and roughened.

The leaves are relatively large and have 5–7 leaflets that all arise from a stout leaf stalk which is 15–20 cm long. Each leaflet may be 6–20 cm long by 4–8 cm wide and their margins are rather coarsely toothed. Each leaflet is on a short stalk or petiolule that is 1–3.5 cm long. *P. colensoi* is the mountain five-finger and typically may have only three leaflets, although some forms do have up to five leaflets. Also, the leaflets of the mountain five-finger have no secondary stalks or petiolules which is how it is distinguished from the common five-finger.

The five-finger flowers are borne in large, compound umbels that are produced from the tips of the branchlets. They are purple in the bud but as they open they become green and are sweetly scented. Flowering usually occurs during June–September. It has purplish-black fruits that are distinctively flattened and are about 5 mm in diameter. A well-fruited tree is most attractive and the fruits are eagerly sought after by various birds, including tui and silvereyes. The fruits usually ripen between August and February.

Five-finger grows in lowland forests and generally ranges from sea level to 760 m. Not infrequently, it can be seen growing as an epiphyte, especially on tree fern trunks, with its roots descending to the ground . It is also known as whauwhaupaku or puahou. In some districts, such as Taranaki, it was formerly known by the unflattering name of snotty-gob, while in Canterbury it used to be known as five-fingered Jack.

Lancewood

Lancewood is a unique New Zealand tree that during its life undergoes a most interesting series of changes. As a juvenile plant it has absolutely no resemblance to the adult tree that it will eventually become.

The first juvenile stage is as a seedling but that soon changes into the longer-lasting phase. This starts with a slender trunk clad with very long leaves resembling ribs of an umbrella that has lost its canopy (see top photo). These leaves are up to 90 cm long by no more than 1–1.25 cm wide and they are strongly deflexed downwards. They are very firm and rigid, being a dark green with yellow or orange midribs and they have toothed margins. This phase can last for up to 15–20 years before the next change commences.

When the tree is ready, the topmost leaves become shorter and broader and they are no longer so strongly deflexed downwards. This may be termed its adolescent stage. Soon afterwards its top may start branching and the leaves become progressively shorter and broader (see lower photo). In the mature or adult phase, the leaves are from 10–20 cm long and may be up to 2–4 cm wide. At this stage the lancewood shows the first signs of developing into a round-headed tree. As the trunk matures, the juvenile leaves drop off, the trunk becomes distinctively fluted and its grey bark is quite smooth. Old trees may be up to 15 m tall and the trunk up to 45 cm in diameter.

As with other members of this family, its green flowers are produced in compound umbels (clusters), usually January–April. Its fruits are more or less globular and are purple when ripe. They can take up to 12 months to ripen, and are eaten by New Zealand pigeons, tui and whiteheads.

Lancewood is common in lowland and lower montane forests throughout the North, South and Stewart Islands, but is absent from the Canterbury Plains and parts of North and Central Otago. It ascends from sea level to 760 m. The wood is dense, even and compact, lightish-brown in colour and sometimes with a satin-like lustre. It was occasionally used for fence posts and piles. It is less commonly known as horoeka. The use of the term lancewood goes back to at least 1872 and derives from the appearance of the juvenile plants.

Toothed lancewood

- Heavily toothed, dark juvenile leaves.
- Smaller than common lancewood.

Height: 6 m

Scientific Name: *Pseudopanax ferox*

The toothed lancewood is similar to the common lancewood but it is usually a smaller tree. It undergoes similar juvenile and semi-adult (adolescent) phases except that its leaves are shorter. The toothed lancewood is distinguished by its heavily toothed semi-juvenile leaves which are usually no more than about 45 cm long (see inset photo). They vary from a dark, blackish-green to a deep olive-green and their midribs are either orange or yellow. These leaves are the tree's most obvious distinguishing character and give rise to its common name.

Adult trees reach a height of no more than about 6 m tall with a small, rounded head. The adult leaves are 7.5–15 cm long by 7–20 mm wide. Their margins either have no teeth or just a few towards their tips. The flowers and fruits are similar to those of lancewood (*P. crassifolius*). The green flowers are produced in compound umbels (clusters), usually January–April. Its fruits are roughly globular and are purple when ripe. Ripening can take up to 12 months, and the fruits are eaten by New Zealand pigeons, tui and whiteheads.

Toothed lancewood has a more scattered distribution throughout the North and South Islands. It occurs in forest and scrub and sometimes in rocky places. In the North Island it occurs from Mangonui southwards. In the South Island it occurs in various scattered localities from Golden Bay to Banks Peninsula, the Rakaia Gorge and central Southland as well as elsewhere. Not infrequently, it is associated with limestone, but also grows in lime-free areas.

Pate

- 3–9 leaflets, thin-textured (unlike five-finger).
- Conspicuous flower panicles.

Height: 8 m

Scientific Name: *Schefflera digitata*

Other Names: (Maori) patete

Pate is usually a small, spreading tree of low stature up to about 8 m tall. It grows throughout the North, South (except the Canterbury Plains) and Stewart Islands where it is not uncommon in lowland and lower montane forests. The species ranges from sea level to 1200 m. Generally, it favours damp parts of the forest such as along stream banks, although it may also be seen as a roadside tree in some areas. With its large, divided leaves it has some resemblance to the five-finger, to which it is related. Usually pate has several stout main stems, their bark being fairly smooth and greyish.

The leaves are on long stalks or petioles up to 25 cm long. There are 3–9 leaflets from 7.5–20 cm long by 3.5–7.5 cm wide. Unlike those of the five-finger, they are not thick and leathery but have a much thinner texture. Each leaflet has a short stalk or petiolule and they have finely toothed margins. The leaves are arranged like the fingers of an outstretched hand. On vigorous, young plants the leaves have a very lush and subtropical appearance.

When it flowers in late summer, the pate is quite spectacular because its much-branched flower panicles are around 20–35 cm across and arise from the branches at irregular intervals. Its flowers are small and greenish and they are followed by small, globular fruits that are dark violet to black when ripe. As with the five-finger, various birds, such as tui, bellbirds and silvereyes, are very fond of the fruits.

The soft wood of the pate was one that was used by Maori for generating fire, by friction. A hard, pointed stick of kaikomako was used to rub into a groove on the pate wood so that, with sufficient effort, enough heat would be generated to kindle some fire. Maori also used the tree's sap to treat ringworm, as it has fungicidal properties.

Pate is also known as patete and on Banks Peninsula it was known as ohau. In some districts it was also known as seven-fingered Jack or seven-finger.

Broadleaf

Broadleaf is one of the most common native trees, occurring throughout most of the North, South and Stewart Islands. It occurs from near the Bay of Islands southwards, but is absent from the Canterbury Plains. Common in lowland and montane forests, it also occurs in lower subalpine scrub and is often a component of open situations such as in rocky places and regenerating scrublands. Broadleaf ranges from sea level to 1060 m. Its scientific name of *littoralis*, which means shore-growing, is misleading because, although it does grow around littoral areas, it is far more common farther inland and even up into mountain areas.

Broadleaf is a rather small tree up to 13–20 m tall, usually much-branched and of a rather spreading habit. Its trunk is often gnarled or twisted and not infrequently it will have several main trunks. On old trees the trunk may be up to 1.5 m in diameter. Its brownish-bark is rough and furrowed.

The leaves are 4–7.5 cm long by 2–3.5 cm wide and their texture is quite thick and leathery, especially when growing in open situations. They are rather shiny on the upper surfaces but not below. Broadleaf's green flowers are quite minute and are produced from the leaf axils in panicles about 2–7.5 cm long. The flowers may be unisexual (separate male and female) on separate trees or some trees may have perfect (male and female combined) flowers. The fleshy fruits are about 7 mm long, and blackish when ripe. They are also eagerly devoured by various native birds.

The wood of the broadleaf is a reddish colour and very durable; the only thing that prevented its greater use being that it is usually very crooked and it was difficult to obtain straight logs of any length. In the early days, large quantities of broadleaf timber were used for farm fencing. In the East Cape district broadleaf is known as papauma while on Stewart Island and in Southland it is known as kapuka. The name broadleaf is the one that is now most generally used throughout New Zealand.

Puka

In contrast to its relative the broadleaf, the puka generally begins life as an epiphyte perched high in some forest tree such as rimu or matai. In spite of its aerial habitat it is a small to medium tree of 8–10 m or so with rather wide-spreading growth. While it is generally epiphytic on other trees, it sometimes grows on the ground.

As an epiphyte, perched up a tree, it gradually commences to send down an aerial root that will eventually reach the ground and so provide the young tree with an increased supply of nourishment. With age, such aerial roots have a corky nature and become quite ridged. The trunk rarely exceeds 30 cm in diameter and its bark is furrowed and uneven, often having a corky appearance.

Its large leaves are quite distinctive, being bright green and glossy. They are 7.5–20 cm long by 6–12.5 cm wide. Apart from its larger leaves, the puka may generally be distinguished from the broadleaf because the bases of the puka leaves are markedly unequal-sided. The leaves of the broadleaf may, at times, be a little unequal but their unequalness cannot be compared with that of the puka's leaves. Puka flowers are not dissimilar to those of the broadleaf, being small, yellowish-green and in panicles produced from the leaf axils. The panicles of male flowers have a showy appearance and are usually longer than the leaves. The female flowers are green and more inconspicuous. The fruits are about 8 mm long and a dark blackish-purple when ripe.

In the North Island the puka occurs in lowland forests from North Cape southwards and it is quite common. In the South Island it is restricted to coastal areas from the Marlborough Sounds and north-western Nelson southwards to Dusky Sound and Foveaux Strait, while in the east it is rare and local along coastal Marlborough. It also occurs on Banks Peninsula.

Puka wood is a light-brown colour and, while compact and very durable, it was seldom available for anything other than occasional use. It used to also be known as akapuka in allusion to its habit of commencing its life perched up in a tree. Aka is a term for species of climbing rata and no doubt the early Maori likened it to a climbing rata.

Mapau

Reddish stems; red leaf stalks.

Leaves dotted with reddish oil glands.

Height: 6 m

Scientific Name: *Myrsine australis*

Other Names: Red matipou; (Maori) mapou, matipou

Mapau is a small tree that has a rather close but superficial resemblance to kohuhu (*Pittosporum tenuifolium*, p. 62), a fact that has been the cause of a certain amount of confusion. Mapau is recognised by its reddish stems or branchlets and its red leaf stalks, whereas kohuhu has blackish stems and green leaf stalks.

Mapau makes a small tree, seldom exceeding 6 m in height, and usually has a rather erect habit. It may have a trunk up to about 30 cm in diameter. The bark on the older parts of the tree is grey or brownish-grey and just slightly roughened.

The leaves are 2.5–6 cm long by 1.5–2.5 cm wide; they have red petioles and undulating margins and they also have a reddish-brown tint. A close examination of the leaves will reveal that they have numerous, minute, reddish oil glands dotted over their upper surfaces. Not infrequently, the leaves are dotted with purplish spots that seem to be an integral feature of the tree and may possibly be a benign fungus that lives on the leaves.

The small whitish flowers are produced in crowded clusters from the leaf axils or on bare branchlets below the leaves. Male and female flowers are on separate trees and flowering usually occurs between December and April, according to district. The small, rounded fruits, about 3 mm in diameter, are black when ripe and attract tui, silvereyes, whiteheads and other birds.

Mapau occurs in lowland and montane forests of the North, South and Stewart Islands but the tree is absent from the Canterbury Plains and parts of North and Central Otago. It ranges from sea level to 900 m.

It is also known as mapou, matipou and red matipou, the last name on account of the reddish colouration of its stems. The old bushmen used to refer it as red maple, the term maple being a corruption of mapou.

- Translucent oil glands on leaves.
- Clusters of small, pinkish flowers.

Height: 9 m

Scientific Name:
Myrsine salicina

As well as being one of the most distinctive of the native species of *Myrsine*, toro is also a most handsome tree. It is not uncommon in the North Island and the northern part of the South Island, occurring in coastal and montane forests from near North Cape southwards. In the South Island it occurs from Golden Bay and north-western Nelson then down Westland to about as far south as Wanganui Bluff. It is absent from the eastern coast of the South Island. It ranges from sea level to about 850 m. When seen in the forest it is quite outstanding as a tree.

Toro usually grows to about 9 m tall and has a rather slender trunk that may be up to 60 cm in diameter. On young trees its bark is smooth and greyish but on older trees it is dark red to almost black, thick and furrowed or roughened. Its branches tend to be rather erect and quite widely spaced.

The spreading leaves are 7.5–17.5 cm long by 2–3 cm wide and are usually produced closer to the ends of the branchlets, and generally held erect. Particularly on the upper surfaces of the leaves, a close examination will reveal a most interesting pattern of translucent, oblong or lineal oil glands, mostly tending to spread out in an oblique fashion from the midrib.

The small, pinkish flowers are produced in dense, many-flowered clusters from below the leaves and along the bare branches. They are usually perfect (male and female in the one flower) and about 3 mm in diameter. Its fruits (see inset photo) may be up to about 9 mm in length and vary from either a reddish colour to an attractive bluish-violet.

Toro wood is a deep red and is attractively figured; its grain is straight and quite strong. Unfortunately, it was never available in sufficient quantity to permit its wide use but it was used by cabinetmakers for both solid wood and as a veneer.

Olearia avicenniifolia

- Bushy shrub or small tree.
- Leaf under-surfaces have buff or white hairs.

Height: 2–6 m

Scientific Name:
Olearia avicenniifolia

Other Names:
(Maori) akeake

While *Olearia avicenniifolia* is one of a number of species of small trees known as akeake, the latter name appears never to have gained currency and so this species is most generally known simply as olearia. It occurs quite widely throughout much of the South and Stewart Islands although it may be rather local in one or two districts. Olearia most commonly grows in lowland to montane scrublands. It will often colonise road banks and other similar places, and ranges from sea level to 900 m.

It is a bushy shrub or small tree that varies from 2 to 6 m tall. In exposed situations it is frequently no more than a small shrub but in more sheltered situations will grow into a much-branched small tree. It sometimes has a short trunk, up to about 40 cm in diameter, but frequently has multiple stems arising straight from the ground. It has pale bark that peels off in quite long strips.

The leaves are 5–10 cm long by 3–5 cm wide; their upper surfaces are medium green with a slight sheen while their undersurfaces have a very tightly interwoven covering of buff or white hairs. The midribs and principal veins are also quite prominent on its undersurfaces.

Olearia flowers during late summer and early autumn and has quite a long flowering period. Its white flowers are borne in flat-topped corymbs and are produced in great profusion. Generally each flower head has only 1–2 ray florets per head.

Akepiro

In some respects akepiro is the North Island equivalent of *Olearia avicenniifolia*. It is a small, much-branched tree reaching around 5 m tall that normally has a short trunk up to about 30 cm in diameter. Its brownish bark peels off in small flakes. Not infrequently, it has no trunk and just produces multiple branches from the ground. Quite often it is no more than a bushy shrub.

Its leaves are 5–10 cm long by 3–6 cm wide and they are a deepish green with a shiny upper surface. Their undersurfaces are clad with a very tightly interwoven covering of buff hairs.

The white flowers are produced from mid-spring to mid-summer in large, flattish corymbs from near the tips of the branchlets. Each daisy-like flower head has up to five ray florets per head.

Akepiro occurs in the North Island in scrublands, along streamsides and around forest margins from near North Cape to the southern Ruahine Range and Taranaki. It is quite common to the north of East Cape and it ranges from sea level to 600 m.

Akepiro is also known as tanguru and wharangipiro.

Heketara

- Profuse clusters of daisy-like flowers.
- Toothed leaves have prominent veins.

Height:
4–8 m

Scientific Name:
Olearia rani

During mid-spring the flowering of the heketara is one of the joys of the North Island forests, as well as those of Nelson and Marlborough. It is a handsome, small, spreading tree 4–8 m tall and often with a short trunk that can be up to 30 cm in diameter. It has thin, greyish-brown bark that does not form an obvious feature of the tree.

The leaves vary from being quite large, 5–15 cm long by 5–6.5 cm wide, to sometimes being quite small and no more than 2.5 cm in length. They have a thin texture, their upper surfaces are green to yellowish-green and they are toothed around their margins. The undersurfaces are white to pale fawn with a dense, close covering of tightly interwoven, fine hairs; the venation is also quite prominent.

Its white flowers are produced in large clusters from near the tips of the branchlets. Each flower head is about 1 cm in diameter and has up to about 12 ray florets. Flowering is generally between September and November during which time the forests are alive with its masses of white.

Heketara must be ranked as one of the most outstanding of the native tree daisies in the North Island, and in the Nelson-Marlborough area it is just as remarkable. It grows in low forest, around forest margins, in clearings, along stream or river banks and in second-growth forest and scrub. Heketara ascends from sea level to about 800 m.

- **Blackish leaf buds.**
- **Leaves dotted with oil glands.**

Height: 3–10 m

Scientific Name: *Myoporum laetum*

Ngaio is a small tree, or sometimes just a shrub, that grows 3–10 m tall. Its trunk may be up to 50 cm or more in diameter and is clad with thick, brown bark that is deeply furrowed. It has quite widely spreading branches.

The leaves are 4–10 cm long by 2–3.5 cm wide with finely toothed margins. The upper surfaces are deep green and shiny and, if the leaves are held up to the light, numerous transparent oil glands can be seen dotted over them. The young leaves, at the branchlet tips, are sticky and the leaf buds have a blackish appearance. The insides of ngaio's white flowers are dotted with purple and also have a beard of coarse, white hairs. They are quite distinctive and arise in clusters of 2–6 from the leaf axils.

For many years, what is commonly referred to as Tasmanian or Australian ngaio (*Myoporum insulare*) has been planted as farm shelter, in coastal areas. This species is now confused with the native ngaio. The Tasmanian ngaio has green leaf buds, not the blackish leaf buds of the native species, but the greatest difference is in the flowers. Tasmanian ngaio's are smaller and only 7–8 mm in diameter with virtually no bearding inside, whereas those of the native species are 10–15 mm in diameter and they are white-bearded inside. The Tasmanian ngaio fruits are only about 6 mm in diameter while those of the native species are generally up to 10 mm long. They vary from pale to dark reddish-purple.

Ngaio is common throughout most of New Zealand, usually in coastal forests, but in some districts may extend some distance inland such as in coastal gorges where air movement prevents damaging frosts. It occurs on the Three Kings Islands and throughout most of the North Island, except the colder inland areas. In the South Island it occurs around coastal areas but becomes rare and local to the south of Dunedin. It is absent from Fiordland. Ngaio ascends from sea level to 450 m.

Ngaio wood is dark brown with black streaks and veining. It is dense, heavy and hard but was only ever used for some speciality purposes and occasionally for fence posts. Early Maori used an infusion of the leaves to wash their faces and other exposed areas of their skin so as to prevent the bites of sandflies and mosquitoes.

Puriri

■ 3–5 large, glossy leaflets.

■ Pinkish-red flowers year-round.

Height: 20 m

Scientific Name: *Vitex lucens*

Puriri is one of New Zealand's noble forest trees, growing to a height of 20 m or so and with a massive trunk of 60 cm–1.5 m in diameter. It has a large, spreading crown and is truly one of the great trees of the forest, being often very long-lived. Its bark is smooth and whitish or yellowish-brown, although with age it may become roughened and furrowed.

It has compound leaves with 3–5 leaflets spreading from a stout stalk 3.5–12.5 cm in length, the two lowermost leaflets being the smallest. The three uppermost leaflets are around 5–12.5 cm long by 3–5 cm wide and they are furrowed along their main veins; their upper surfaces are deep green and shiny, and they have entire (untoothed) margins.

The pinkish-red puriri flowers are very attractive, being produced in great abundance on branched panicles that come from the axils of the leaves. Each flower is 2.5–3.5 cm in diameter. There is hardly a time of the year when a puriri tree does not have flowers on it, and their nectar is popular with bellbirds, silvereyes and tui. Its fleshy fruits are rounded, about 2 cm in diameter and bright red when ripe. About the only native bird capable of swallowing a puriri fruit is the New Zealand pigeon.

Puriri is common in the upper North Island, in coastal and lowland forests, from near North Cape to the Waikato region and upper Thames and then of local occurrence southwards to the Mahia Peninsula and Cape Egmont. It ranges from sea level to 760 m.

Puriri wood is dark reddish-brown, very heavy and dense. It used to be one of our most valuable hardwoods. It was formerly used for house blocks, piles, railway sleepers and other construction purposes. Unfortunately, the wood is often spoiled by caterpillars that tunnel into the trunk, leaving quite large holes. They are caused by the larvae of the puriri moth (*Hepialus virescens*), a large, green and very attractive native moth. It is interesting that when old trees were milled the wood was so hard that it was sometimes necessary to use explosives to split it. The tree was occasionally also known as kauere and its usual name of puriri was sometimes corrupted to puri.

Mangrove

Mangrove is, in some ways, one of the most ignored trees in New Zealand. Many people feel that mangrove swamps are ugly or unimportant and do not realise the vital functions that they perform in the ecology of estuaries, harbours and inlets.

The mangrove varies from a small, much-branched tree up to 15 m tall, in the warmest parts of the north, to a small shrub maybe no more than about 50 cm tall, or less, at its southernmost limit. Its grey bark is furrowed and somewhat roughened. Its branches are usually stout.

Its root system is quite remarkable, especially the peg-like aerial roots that project out of the mud at low tide (lower photo). They are known as pneumatophores and they enable the tree's root system to obtain the oxygen that it cannot otherwise access from the estuarine mud.

The thick, leathery leaves are 5–10 cm long by 2–4 cm wide, shiny on their upper surfaces while their undersurfaces are whitish or buff-coloured. Its small flowers are produced during February and April in clusters of 4–8 on erect, angled stalks. The seeds take until the following January to ripen and are remarkable because each is formed in a leathery capsule about 2 cm long and while it is still hanging on the tree it forms a small root that projects outside the capsule so that is virtually an embryonic plant in waiting. When the seed capsule finally falls it drops into the water and floats until deposited in the mud by an outgoing tide so that it is able to root in immediately before being washed away by the next incoming tide. These mangrove seeds (or seedlings) are able to drift on the tide and survive for several weeks until attaching themselves to the mud.

Mangroves naturally occur from North Cape southwards to about Kawhia on the west coast and Ohiwa Harbour on the east coast. It is interesting to observe the gradual decrease in the height of mangroves from north to south. In the far north they attain their maximum height, at about Puhoi they may be around 3 m tall and south of Auckland their height rapidly decreases until they are no more than 30–50 cm at their southern limit. Mangrove is also known as manawa and it was also formerly known as white mangrove.

Cabbage tree

- Tufts of sword-like leaves.
- Large panicles of flowers.

Height: 4–12 m

Scientific Name: *Cordyline australis*

Other Names: (Maori) ti-kouka

As well as being one of the commonest of our native trees the cabbage tree may be regarded as perhaps the most iconic. It is very distinctive and is seen in many different situations, varying from swamps to forest margins and on barren, windswept hillsides. It occurs throughout the North, South and Stewart Islands, ranging from sea level to 760 m.

When young, the cabbage tree grows on a slender, unbranched stem and, at that stage, usually has much longer leaves than the adult tree. After its first flowering, the tree begins to branch because the flower panicle arises from the growing tip, thus causing its trunk to branch. From that point onwards, each successive flowering causes further branching.

Throughout the country cabbage trees vary considerably in size, ranging 4–12 m in height. Those in the far north often have several slender trunks, whereas further south they often have just one larger trunk. The trunk may be 10 cm–1.5 m in diameter with thick, rough, corky bark.

The leaves are 30–90 cm long by 3–6 cm wide. Generally, both surfaces are similar green colour, but some trees may show glaucousness or greyish colour. When in flower from late spring the tree is at its most spectacular. Large flowering panicles (see inset photo), 60 cm–1.2 m long, bear numerous small, white or creamy-white flowers that are very sweetly scented; on a fine day their scent pervades the air. The white or bluish fruits are about 7 mm in diameter and berry-like. They are eagerly eaten by birds, including bellbirds and New Zealand pigeons.

The name of cabbage tree dates to 1769 and Captain Cook's first voyage to New Zealand, when members of his expedition referred to the nikau palm as cabbage tree or cabbage palm. This name soon came to also refer to *Cordyline australis*, so that by the time the first European settlers arrived it was used almost exclusively as a common name for the *Cordyline*. To Maori it is known as ti-kouka as well as quite a number of similar variants, all with the prefix 'ti', a generic term for species of *Cordyline*.

The pith of the trunk as well as its fleshy root once provided a sought-after food item for Maori, as did the young leaf bud. Since the time of Cook's voyage, its edible leaf bud was also used by Europeans.

Nikau palm

New Zealand's only native palm is an elegant and graceful tree that gives a decided subtropical air to many areas in the warmer parts of New Zealand. It is very easily recognised with its feather duster-like appearance.

Nikau grows to about 10 m tall and its trunk is 15–24 cm in diameter. As with one or two other trees, nikau palms growing in the far north often appear to have thinner trunks than those growing further south. The trunks are ringed with the scars of its fallen fronds and are usually smooth and green except on older trees when they become grey and somewhat roughened.

The fronds are up to 3 m long and they have very broad sheathing bases that give the top of the trunk its bulbous appearance. The flowers are on a large inflorescence and arise from just below the bases of the fronds. They are at first encased in a pair of large, boat-shaped casings known as spathes. After these spathes split open, the inflorescence, 30–60 cm long, is then able to expand, allowing its densely crowded pinkish flowers to open. The fruits (see inset photo) are bright red and very colourful. At first they are more or less pointed at both ends but as they ripen they tend to become more rounded. The fruits are a favourite food of New Zealand pigeons and kaka.

Nikau occurs in lowland and hilly forests throughout most of the North Island and in the South Island in coastal forests as far south as Banks Peninsula in the east and to Wanganui Bluff in the west. It also occurs on the Chatham Islands, and along with those on the Banks Peninsula site, enjoys the distinction of being the southernmost palm in the world.

The unexpanded leaf bud, at the top of the trunk, is edible and was eaten by early Maori. It was also eaten by members of Captain Cook's 1769 expedition to New Zealand who first coined the name of cabbage tree for it (see notes under *Cordyline australis*, p. 162). Some of the early European settlers also ate the young leaf buds. Of course, doing so effectively destroys the whole tree. Both Maori and early European settlers used the fronds for cladding whares and bushmen's huts, while strips from the frond were also used for weaving baskets. The very hard seeds were sometimes used for bird shooting when ammunition was in short supply.

Silver tree fern

- Silvery undersides to fronds.

- Trunk base fibrous, upper part has old frond stalks.

Height: 10 m

Scientific Name: *Cyathea dealbata*

Other Names: (Maori) ponga

The source of our national emblem, the silver tree fern is one of the most distinct and easily recognised of our native tree ferns. Just a look at the silvery undersides of its fronds is sufficient to identify it (see inset photo).

Silver tree fern grows to about 10 m tall and has a rather thick trunk up to about 45 cm in diameter. Like the nikau and one or two other trees, when growing in the far north the silver tree fern may often have a trunk that is thinner than is usual for this species. The base of the trunk is fibrous with old aerial roots, while the upper part of the trunk is marked by the bases of the stalks of the old fronds.

It has numerous fronds that usually spread more or less horizontally to form quite a large crown. The fronds are 2–4 m long by 60 cm–1.2 m wide, and the bases of the frond stalks are usually covered with a silvery-white, waxy bloom. On very young plants the undersurfaces of the fronds are green and it may take several years for the typical silvery-white appearance to properly develop. The undersurfaces of its fertile fronds are liberally dotted with numerous brown sori (clusters of spore-containing structures) which are like tiny raised blisters. They produce and release the spores that may give rise to young tree ferns.

Silver tree fern occurs throughout most of the North Island in lowland and montane forests. In the South Island it occurs to about as far south as the Catlins area on the east coast and it is probably absent from most of the west coast area. It is also absent from the Canterbury Plains, North and Central Otago, although it does occur on Banks Peninsula.

The Maori name for the silver tree fern is ponga. Unfortunately, nowadays people tend to use this name for any species of tree fern, regardless of which one. Over the years, ponga has also been corrupted to a variety of other names varying from punga to bungie, the latter variant having originated with the old-time bushmen.

Mamaku

- Tall, slender trunk.

- Large crown of 20–30 fronds.

Height: 8–20 m

Scientific Name:
Cyathea medullaris

Other Names:
Black tree fern, king fern (Westland)

Mamaku is the tallest of our tree ferns and, in some respects, the most magnificent. It has a tall, slender trunk that often appears to be too thin to support its large crown of fronds. It is very easily recognised; a passing glance usually being sufficient to identify it.

Mamaku will grow 8–20 m or more tall and some specimens may be even taller. The base of the trunk is around 30 cm in diameter, being built out with fibrous roots, but higher up the trunk can be quite slender.

There may be 20–30 fronds in its crown, which are slightly curving or arching and are 2.5–6 m long by up to 2 m wide. Their upper surfaces are dark green and shining while the undersurfaces are paler. The undersurfaces of fertile fronds are dotted with myriad dark-brown sori (clusters of spore-containing structures).

Mamaku is found from sea level to about 600 m and occurs in lowland and hilly forests throughout the North Island, where it can be extremely plentiful in some districts. In the South Island it occurs from the Marlborough Sounds and Nelson, down the west coast to southern Fiordland; on the eastern coast it occurs sparingly in eastern Marlborough, in eastern Otago and is rare on Banks Peninsula. It also occurs on Stewart Island. The mamaku is often very plentiful in pine plantations and also on recently cleared land where it often grows to the exclusion of almost anything else. Mamaku is also known as black tree fern and in Westland it is known as the king fern.

- Thick, fibrous trunk
- Skirt of old fronds at top of trunk.

Height: 8 m

Scientific Name: *Cyathea smithii*

Other Names: Soft tree fern; (Maori) katote

Whe is a beautiful tree fern that occurs in damp lowland and montane forests in the North, South and Stewart Islands from Kaitaia southwards. It is absent from the Canterbury Plains, North and Central Otago. In addition whe occurs on the Chatham Islands. It also has the distinction of having the southernmost distribution of any tree fern in New Zealand, and probably in the world, because it occurs on the remote subantarctic Auckland Islands. While it does not stand much exposure to the harsh elements, it is the only tree fern to venture so far south. It ranges from sea level to 600 m and may be the dominant tree fern in forest at higher altitudes.

Whe grows to a height of about 8 m and it has a rather thick fibrous trunk up to about 24 cm in diameter. The one character by which it may be recognised is the skirt or investment of the old frond midribs that adorns the top of its trunk. The old fronds die and just hang downwards, without falling off, but in the process everything else falls off them or disintegrates, just leaving the stalks or midribs hanging there. That alone, together with its fibrous trunk, is sufficient to identify it.

The fronds have a very soft texture and actually appear to be quite delicate. They spread horizontally and are 1.5–2.7 m long by 45–75 cm wide. They are a lovely bright, fresh green colour and are paler on their undersurfaces. The stalks of its fronds are furnished with pale to dark-brown chaffy scales which are another means of identifying it.

On the fertile fronds numerous small and dark-brown sori (clusters of spore-containing structures) appear to cover the undersurface. Whe is also known as soft tree fern and katote.

- Slender black trunk covered with bases of old stalks.
- Top of trunk often has skirt of old fronds.

Height: 6 m

Scientific Name:
Dicksonia squarrosa

Apart from the mamaku, wheki is probably the most abundant of our native tree ferns and is found in forest areas throughout most of the country. It is common in lowland and hilly forests throughout the North, South and Stewart Islands, as well as the Chatham Islands, and it ranges from sea level to 760 m.

Wheki grows to a height of about 6 m and its trunk is about 10–15 cm in diameter. Occasionally, specimens with thicker trunks may be encountered; however, its generally slender, black trunk clad with the rigid, black bases of the old fronds, projecting upwards, is usually sufficient to identify it. If there is any doubt, the top of its trunk is often (but not always) girdled with a dense skirt or investment of old fronds which will be sufficient to confirm its identification.

The fronds of the wheki are 1.2–2.4 m long by 60 cm–1 m wide. Their upper surfaces are dark green and they are distinctly paler beneath. Its fronds have a very harsh and rough texture. The undersurfaces of the fertile fronds are so densely covered with sori (clusters of spore-containing structures) that they cause the margins of the frond segments to strongly roll downwards. Its black frond stalks (see inset photo) are densely clad with coarse, long, brownish-black hairs.

In cleared areas of forest wheki is quick to regenerate and often whole groves or colonies of it may be seen in such areas. It is one of the few native tree ferns that is able to put forth underground rhizomes that will produce new plants, thus enabling it to form colonies.

Bibliography

Allan, H.H., *Flora of New Zealand*, Vol. 1, Government Printer: Wellington, 1961.

Cave, Y. & Paddison, V., *The Gardener's Encyclopaedia of New Zealand Native Plants*, Godwit: Auckland, 1999.

Dawson, J. & Lucas, R., *Nature Guide to the New Zealand Forest*, Godwit: Auckland, 2000.

Eagle, A., *Eagle's Trees and Shrubs of New Zealand*, Collins: Auckland, 1978.

Metcalf, L.J., *New Zealand Trees and Shrubs*, Reed: Auckland, 2000.

Moore, L.B. & Edgar, E., *Flora of New Zealand*, Vol. 2, Government Printer: Wellington, 1970.

Mortimer, J. & Mortimer, B., *Trees for the New Zealand Countryside*, Taitua Books: Rotorua, 1999.

Poole, L. & Adams, N.M., *Trees and Shrubs of New Zealand*, Department of Scientific and Industrial Research: Wellington, 1994.

Porteus, T., *Native Forest Restoration*, Queen Elizabeth II National Trust: Wellington, 1993.

Salmon, J.T., *The Native Trees of New Zealand*, Reed: Auckland, 1997.

Simpson, P. *Dancing Leaves*, Canterbury University Press: Christchurch, 2000.

Index